THE JEWISH YEAR

CELEBRATING THE HOLIDAYS

STEWART, TABORI & CHANG

THE JEWISH YEAR
CELEBRATING THE HOLIDAYS

Barbara Rush

A FAIR STREET/WELCOME BOOK

Stewart, Tabori & Chang

NEW YORK

CONTENTS

ABOVE: *The Feast of Purim*, Marc Chagall, 1973.
Collection of Chagall, Saint Paul-de-Vence,
France/Scala/Art Resource, NY. ©2000 Artists Rights
Society (ARS), New York/ADAGP, Paris.

PAGE ONE: *Zodiac Wheel of Fortune*, Abraham Judah ben
Yehiel of Camerino from the *Rothschild Mahzor*
(Ms. 8892, fol. 52), Italy, 1492. Courtesy of The Library
of the Jewish Theological Seminary of America.

PAGE TWO: *Succot*, David Sharir, 1981.
Courtesy Pucker Gallery, Boston.

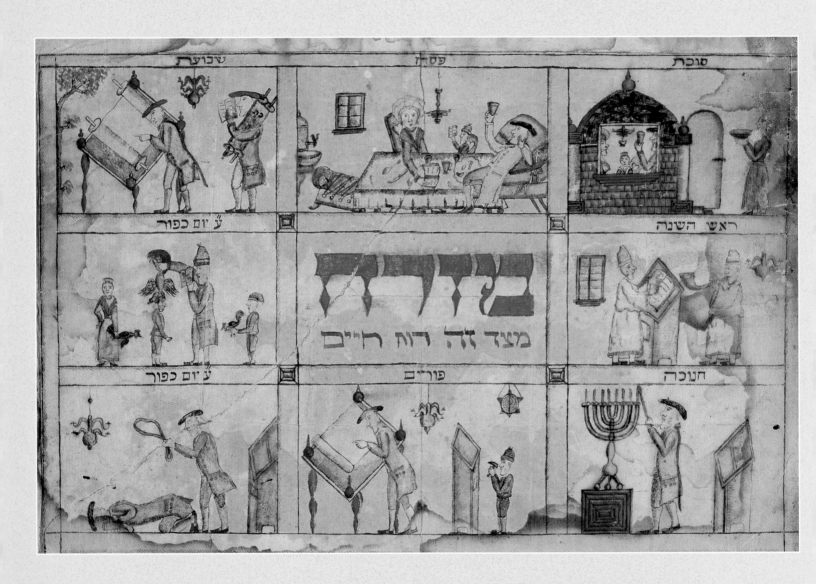

INTRODUCTION

Mizrach ("East") with Jewish Holidays, Germany, 18th century. Israel Museum, Jerusalem/ Erich Lessing/ Art Resource, NY.

The Jewish people are blessed with festivals—days that are purposeful, special, and sacred, and that occur and are renewed in an unending cycle. For thousands of years all over the world, Jews have observed these special times that commemorate historic events, celebrate nature and the harvest, and inspire renewal of the spirit. Throughout the year, in Jewish households, these ancient festivals—and modern holidays as well—represent the thread that binds and unites all Jewish people. On these days one finds joy and thankfulness in the blessedness of God's world—and having done so, shares these blessings with others.

The festivals of the Jewish year take place in Jewish sacred time, as opposed to profane time, those days of the year when festivals are not celebrated. Some holidays, such as Rosh Hashanah, Yom Kippur, Sukkot, Chanukah, Purim, Pesach, and Shavuot, are celebrated annually; another, Rosh Chodesh, follows the rhythm of the month, guided by the waxing and waning of the moon. As in biblical times, the sighting of each new moon is blessed today. And the Sabbath, imbued with its own spirit of holiness, crowns each of the month's four weeks of seven days. Each day of the week, in fact, has its own sacred rhythm, manifested in morning and afternoon-evening prayers.

Many traditions and stories link these sacred times of the festivals with Jewish sacred spaces, primarily the Land of Israel and its capital, Jerusalem. The synagogue, too, is holy, sanctified by prayer; the cemetery, where the body is laid to rest and where prayers are recited, is also hallowed; and so is the home, protected by the mezuzah, which conceals a parchment containing the Divine Name on its doors. Just as sacred space and sacred time are intertwined, one festival may be tied to another. And woven into many festivals are also the rituals of weddings, funerals, and other parts of the cycle of life.

The Jewish year is a multi-dimensional tapestry, composed of holidays that range in date of origin from three thousand to thirty-five years ago. Some celebrations last one day, others are eight; some are solemn and reverent in mood, others fun and filled with frivolity; some days are celebrated primarily at home, while others are observed mostly in the synagogue.

The festivals derive from different historical periods. During biblical times, hundreds of thousands of people would gather at the Holy Temple in Jerusalem—the Temple of Solomon—on Pesach, Shavuot, and Sukkot to celebrate God-given moments in history: the Exodus from Egypt, the receiving of the Torah at Sinai, and the forty years of wandering to the Land of Israel.

The year 586 B.C.E. marked a turning point in Jewish history: the Temple was destroyed, and the Jews were led in captivity to Babylonia. With no homeland, no Holy Temple, and no sacrifices, how could Jewish life continue? The answer came in the development of the community synagogue, in lieu of the Temple, as a place for Jews to congregate and pray. Less than a century later, the Persian king captured Babylonia and allowed the Jews to return and rebuild the Temple. Once again Jews flocked to Jerusalem for their major festivals.

About 332 B.C.E. Alexander the Great, whose domain included nearby Greece, conquered the Near East. For the Jews of Palestine, the nearly two centuries that followed were marked by the assimilation of Greek culture and language, and the eventual rise of oppressive rulers. The festival of Chanukah celebrates the overthrow of these rulers in 165 B.C.E.

Subsequently, the oppressive reign of Rome usurped the practice of Jewish life and eventually destroyed the Second Temple in 70 C.E. Those Jews who remained later rebelled against Roman rule; the holiday of Lag B'Omer commemorates those valiant leaders.

But most Jews were dispersed, this time to the Diaspora—not only to Babylonia, where a large community grew and flourished, but throughout the Roman Empire, which later came under Christian and Muslim rule. The question persisted: "How can Jewish life and culture survive?" The answer came in the form of midrash—stories created by the rabbis to explain and interpret the Bible—and in the completion of two Talmuds—one in Palestine and one in Babylonia—by 500 C.E. These works, comprising a vast collection of rabbinic law and lore, brought new interpretations to the festivals and gave the Jewish people specific instructions on how to observe them.

In later centuries, Jewish communities and scholarship continued to thrive, despite anti-Semitic edicts, expulsions, and pogroms. The sixteenth-century mystics of Safed in northern Israel left a legacy of beautiful customs, such as the welcoming of the Sabbath Bride with song. In eighteenth-century Poland, Rabbi Israel ben Eliezer—called the Baal Shem Tov—founded Chasidism; many beautiful Chasidic stories and customs survive in our celebrations today. The rise of Zionism in the nineteenth century, as well as the founding of the modern State of Israel in the aftermath of the Holocaust in the twentieth, provided new occasions for holidays and celebrations.

A knowledge of Jewish history leads one not only to appreciate Judaism and its legacy, but also to decide, "Where shall I go, how shall I celebrate, in the future?" In this book, the history of each holiday is recounted. Because the Jews, throughout their long history, never lived in an environment entirely separate from their non-Jewish neighbors, many Jewish festivals were adapted from those of pagans, Christians, and Muslims. But Judaism cast its own Jewish form on each festival, imbuing each observance with a Jewish ethic; for instance, Purim, the carnival-like spring festival, became a time to share food with the poor. Historically, it is also the Jewish way to turn despair into salvation, gloom into hope; thus, the solemn mood of remembering Israel's fallen soldiers turns into the happy celebration of the country's independence.

The basis of almost every Jewish festival is the observance of religious law called *halachah*, Hebrew for "the path." These laws are set down in the Torah (the first five books of the Bible), in which Jewish belief is grounded, as well as in the Talmud (the second most sacred Jewish text after the Bible), and the Shulchan Aruch (the most important code of Jewish law). For every festival there are specific dictates of religious law that are mandatory and inflexible. Every word of a Torah portion, for instance, read on Sabbath or other festivals, is fixed; not even one word may be changed. Various religious communities, however, differ in what they consider religious law or what they believe obligatory for observance.

How a people observes a holiday has to do also with how it embellishes, embroiders, and enhances the law with creativity, with unique expressions of art and craft, food and dress, dance and song, story and proverb. These individual expressions eventually become customs: eating a braided white bread on Sabbath, singing special songs on Chanukah, and placing a distinctive plate on the Passover table. Every custom is based on belief, some known, others long forgotten; but the custom remains and is always a central part of the celebration.

What we eat, how we dress, what we sing, what we tell—these combine to become the lore of the people. Folk customs, full of beauty and meaning, do not replace religious law but rather supplement and enrich it; they are expressions of what the great family of Jews around the world have passed down from generation to generation, voluntarily and without the mandate of religious law. Such customs are not fixed: a recipe may change according to the taste of the cook; a story may change according to the creativity of the teller. A uniqueness of this volume is that it includes and explains festival celebrations as seen through the actions and performed according to the wishes of the folk.

No festival is entirely religious or entirely secular. Every celebration is a combination of both

religious roots and folk embellishment: Holocaust Remembrance Day, a twentieth-century secular holiday, includes prayer as part of its celebration. Conversely, even the holiest day of Yom Kippur is lightened with humorous folktales.

In addition to the obvious ways of marking festive occasions (adding artistic decoration, wearing special clothes, eating special food, singing appropriate songs), people weave into their observance imaginative "ways" and "devices" that make the celebration even more meaningful or sacred. For example, on the holiday of Purim Jews eat a cake filled with poppy seeds; the German/Yiddish word for poppy seeds is *mohn*, which sounds like the second syllable of Haman, a central character in the Purim story.

Numbers, as well the sounds of words, add significance to our customs. In secular celebrations, we customarily add an extra good-luck candle to the ones on a birthday cake. In religious celebration, Jews often use the number seven, such as the seven biblical heroes who are invited to eat in the sukkah. The number seven is associated with holiness and completion: the world was completed in seven days, ending with the day of Sabbath rest; and the special year, when the land must lie fallow and debt is forgiven, occurs every seventh year. The action of circling is also woven into many festivals, as when the synagogue is circled seven times at the end of Sukkot. The circle, an ancient and universal magical symbol, is believed to protect those within its borders from evil spirits.

In addition, people love to make use of "number magic," a mental exercise called *gematria*, in which each letter of the Hebrew alphabet has a numerical equivalent, and each Hebrew word represents the sum of its letters' numerical values. For example, the Hebrew word *chai*, meaning "life," is comprised of the numerical equivalents of 8 and 10. Thus, many Jews give gifts in the amount of 18 dollars, because this sum, they believe, will bring long life.

Many customs derive from ancient, Talmudic, or medieval beliefs that lurking demons, jealous of humans and ready to attack, were prevalent. People devised tactics—often similar to those used for fighting visible enemies—to rid their daily lives of these invisible spirits: frontal attacks of light and noise, gifts meant to placate the enemy, or compromise. Lighting candles, singing loudly, stamping feet on Purim, clinking glasses, and leaving wine for Elijah the Prophet (a good spirit) on Pesach are typical of the anti-demonic "weapons" that have become part of present-day celebration. These and other "ways" of the folk will be noted and explained in festivals throughout this book.

Since the time of the initial covenant at Sinai— made in writing—between God and the Jewish people, both written and oral literature have passed down our Jewish cultural heritage. *The Jewish Year* offers written literature depicting the richness and diversity of festival celebration. Selections from ancient sources, examples of modern midrash (interpretations of passages in the Bible), and personal memories recounted by Peninnah Schram and other fine storytellers enrich this book; so, too, do the writings of masters of Jewish literature Sholom Aleichem and H. N. Bialik; Nobel laureates

I. B. Singer, S. J. Agnon, and Elie Wiesel; and the poetry of Yehuda Amichai.

In this volume, too, are folktales, retold by Howard Schwartz, Rabbi Zalman Schacter-Shalomi, and other renowned storytellers in the United States. Folktales—stories handed down orally from one generation to another—represent the memory and soul of the Jewish people. Holiday tales, especially, reflect the faith and ethics maintained by Jews throughout the centuries, often despite pending destruction by their enemies. Many selections are from the Israel Folktale Archives (IFA), whose holdings include more than 22,000 tales collected in Israel from various ethnic groups.

Throughout the centuries, art, too, has played an important role in festival celebration. These pages are filled with exquisite examples, drawn from the traditions of depicting stories from the Bible, of illuminating manuscripts, of creating folk art, and of fashioning sacred ceremonial objects—such as the eight-branched Chanukah candelabra—that have, for centuries, beautified and heightened Jewish religious experience. In this book, in addition to manuscript pages and elaborate Torah ornaments, we find a New Year's greeting card carved into a walrus tusk in Alaska and a Passover bag for holding matzah, delicately crafted in China. This international range of art attests to the importance of holiday observance to Jews everywhere; along with the stories and poetry, the artwork captures the spirit and tradition of celebrating throughout the year.

By introducing the reader to a wide variety of Jewish communities, *The Jewish Year* instills the sense that all belong to *k'lal Yisrael*, the enormous family of Jews around the globe. Their celebrations are enriched by special Jewish languages, usually a mixture of Hebrew plus the vernacular: Yiddish, Ladino, or one of the many dialects of Judeo-Arabic or Judeo-Persian. The spectrum of Jews worldwide may be divided as follows: Ashkenazi—or Ashkenazic—Jews, hailing largely from western, central, and Eastern Europe; Sephardi—or Sephardic—Jews, whose ancestors, expelled from the Iberian Peninsula 500 years ago, settled on the shores of the Mediterranean, in the Balkans, North Africa, and even northern Europe and the Land of Israel; and Mizrachi—also called Eastern or Oriental—Jews, most of whose families came from Islamic countries. Other Jews hail from Ethiopia, India, and, in the past, China. Some—Samaritans and Karaites—were or are bound together by their common adherence only to the Torah or the entire Bible, not to later rabbinic interpretations. (In popular vernacular, some people use the term *Sephardic* for all Jews who are not of Ashkenazic background.)

If you have you ever wondered why Jews prepare two braided Sabbath loaves and not three on Friday night, or why Jews eat a round bread, studded with raisins, on Rosh Hashanah, the new year festival; if you want to know what prayers and blessings to recite on particular holidays or how to celebrate at home and in the synagogue; or if you have forgotten the sights and sounds, the tastes and smells of your childhood—the aroma of Grandma's *bimuelos* or Grandpa's latkes, the flickering of Chanukah lights, the blasting of the ram's horn on New Year—*The Jewish Year* will answer your questions and

rekindle your memories. Its pages will help you conjure the festivals of your past and inspire you to incorporate the traditions of other Jewish communities into your own.

Use this book to enrich your celebrations or create them anew. Because there is no single interpretation of the meaning of any festival, draw upon the multiple sources—religious laws, folk customs, historic events, the seasons of nature—that give each holiday a unique character and flavor.

Whether you are relatively new to festival celebration or familiar with a holiday's observance, this volume will guide you as you journey through the Jewish year. Begin with one festival: dip in, taste a bit of the celebration, and enjoy! Let the art, literature, and observances presented here exhilarate you with the joy and beauty of the legacy that is the Jewish year.

A NOTE ON HEBREW AND TRANSLITERATION
There is no perfect system for translating Hebrew vowels into English. In general, the English a or ah sound = the ah sound in Hebrew; e or eh = eh; ei = ay or ai; i = ee; o = oh; ai = ah + ee, a combination that does not exist in English. We have used ch to reflect the guttural sound of the Hebrew letters chaf and chet, as in baruch and Chanukah. And we have chosen the Sephardic Hebrew pronunciation used in Israel for most Hebrew words (Sukkot, Shabbat), except for plurals, which we have formed by adding s, as in seder/seders. The writings of contributing authors retain the transliteration system used when their work was originally printed.

I have a precious gift in my treasure house, and Sabbath is its name. I wish to present it to Israel.
—BABYLONIAN TALMUD, SHAB. 10B

THE SABBATH

After a week of toil, can anything be more joyous than to welcome, with hymns and with song, a special Sabbath Queen or Bride, who arrives on Sabbath eve? As the words of a Sabbath song tell us, "And with her come angels with peace and with blessing." What could be more peaceful than a day when the Gates of Hell are closed, and evil has no power? And what could be more fortunate than to receive an additional soul, given by God to every person, that invigorates one all day until Sabbath departs? According to Jewish tradition, these pleasures are just some of the precious gifts that accompany the Sabbath. This special day, the mystics thought, is simply a foretaste of the bliss awaiting the righteous in the World to Come.

The Sabbath as a day of rest is a gift that Jews have given to the world. Many other ancient cultures, especially those in Asia and Africa, observed a day without routine work, but used the time to take goods to market; or, work was suspended on days considered to be connected to unlucky phases of the moon. The Jewish contribution, however, has established a day of rest that truly restricts labor of humans and beasts and is celebrated with joy—a time of holiness each week throughout the year.

The Sabbath has a long history, going back to the very beginning of the Torah: Genesis 1:1 and 2:3 tell us that God worked for six days at creating the world and rested on the seventh day, blessing the day and declaring it holy. But the word "Sabbath," related to the Hebrew verb *shavat*—"to rest, to cease, to desist"—is not mentioned. In Exodus 16:13-29, after God supplies the wandering Children of Israel with wonderful dew-covered food (manna) for five days, they are sent a double portion on the sixth day because no food will arrive on the seventh day. Similarly, when they later go about gathering food, the Israelites are told to prepare a double portion on the sixth day, so they can rest from the labor of gathering food on the seventh. In this portion of the Torah, this seventh day is called a "Sabbath of the Lord," a designation that implies its sanctity and blessedness. Finally, in Exodus 31:16, the covenant with God is established, and Jews are commanded to "keep the Sabbath, to observe the Sabbath throughout their generations, for a perpetual covenant." The fourth commandment states: "Remember the Sabbath day and keep it holy: six days you shall labor and do all your work; but the seventh day is a Sabbath of the Lord your God: you shall not do any work, you, your son or daughter, your male or female slave, or your cattle, or the stranger who is within your settlements."

In Isaiah 58:13, the Sabbath is called a delight. Indeed, in the days of the First Temple in Jerusalem, before 586 B.C.E., it was a day to cease daily work and

Sabbath Table,
Malcah Zeldis, 1996.
Private Collection/
Malcah Zeldis/
Art Resource, NY.

A Day of Rest, a Day of Delight

also a day to gather in Jerusalem for joyous celebration. And so, based on biblical instruction, the tradition of the Sabbath as a day of rest and joy was interpreted and reinterpreted for many years.

After the destruction of the First Temple in 586 B.C.E., during the exile in Babylonia, the Sabbath really developed, because it fit the circumstances of exile. Observing a day of rest distinguished Jews from their neighbors, and the observance of Sabbath contributed to the development of the synagogue, where Jews could pray together and spend the day in religious study. Even today the synagogue is the place where, on the Sabbath, Jews hear the Torah, every word of which is prescribed by religious law; the Torah is so holy that it may be written only by specially trained scribes.

The Book of Exodus forbids work on the Sabbath, upon penalty of death. The Mishnah, a third-century codification of the laws of the Torah upon which the Talmud is based, lists thirty-nine specific actions that are forbidden, such as sowing, plowing, hammering, kindling, and extinguishing. Generations of rabbis have since added further refinements, and modern technology has made it easier for Jews to keep religious commandments. For example, at home, electric timers eliminate the need even to throw a switch or plug in an appliance on the Sabbath. According to the Jewish sages, the Sabbath is made for people, not people for the Sabbath; Sabbath regulations may and should be broken in case of danger to health. The Sabbath, and the concept of work, mean different things to different people; but for everyone, it is a day to rest in a specifically Jewish way.

Then what is the purpose of the Sabbath? Certainly it is intended as a cessation from work and a day of joy, but ultimately, it is even more than that: because God created the world in six days, rested on the seventh, and was refreshed (Exodus 31:17), so too should every person be refreshed by this day of spiritual reflection. The Sabbath is a time of holiness—a day that inspires and ennobles one's soul. The best of everything comes out on the Sabbath: the finest food, dress, and dinnerware; the most joyous songs; the most sacred objects and treasured heirlooms. The many beautiful customs that families share on this day give the Sabbath an aura of holiness that is almost indescribable.

At home, preparations for the Sabbath (*Shabbat* in Hebrew; *Shabbos* in Yiddish) begin on Thursday and continue on Friday with shopping, cleaning, and cooking. Then, at nightfall on Friday, the many ceremonies that receive and welcome the Sabbath begin.

Jews usher in the festival by lighting at least two candles, often set on a white cloth (for purity), that

Dressed Torah Scroll. Torah Mantle: Prussia, 18th century. Pair of Rimmonim: Berlin, 1788-1802. Torah Pointer: Danzig Jewish Community, 1766-1812. The Jewish Museum, New York/Art Resource, NY.

Blessings recited over wine, bread, and candlelight express thanks for these God-given gifts. Each blessing begins with a direct address to God: Baruch Atah Adonai, Eloheinu Melech Ha'olam—"Praised be our Eternal God, Ruler of the Universe." These opening words are followed by phrases that complete the blessing and make it specific:

(over wine): Borei pri hagafen—*"Creator of the fruit of the vine"*

(over bread): Hamotzi lechem min ha'aretz—*"Who brings forth bread from the earth"*

(over candlelight): Asher kid'shanu b'mitzvotav v'tzivanu l'hadlik ner shel Shabbat—*"Who hallows us with commandments and commands us to kindle the Sabbath lights."*

are traditionally kindled by the mother in the family, although men may light them too. The blessing of the Sabbath candles, *Ner shel Shabbat*, is recited. As the woman lights the candles, she shields her eyes with her hands, because once she recites the blessing, it is Sabbath; and if it's Sabbath, she's not allowed to kindle; the shielding separates the blessing from the kindling. Beautiful candlesticks of brass or silver are often handed down as treasures from one generation to another. There are usually two candles, although the reasons for this number remain unknown. Perhaps one stands for charity, and one stands for Shabbat finery. Maybe one stands for the first part of the fourth commandment, "Remember the Sabbath day," and one stands for the second part, "and keep it holy." Perhaps one is for man and one is for woman, because Shabbat eve is the time when a husband and wife should "be fruitful and multiply," as God commanded Adam and Eve (Genesis 1:28). Perhaps there is one candle for each of the two hot servings of the meal. There may be more than two candles; in some families a light is kindled for each family member.

Next, Jews recite the blessing over the wine, *Borei pri hagafen*. An especially beautiful cup—the

kiddush or holy cup—made of fine glass or precious metal, holds the wine. After the blessing, the kiddush cup is passed around so that each person may take a sip; or each person sips from his or her own cup after clinking glasses with others at the table, and saying, "*L'chaim*—To life."

The Sabbath observance continues with the blessing and eating of a special bread called challah, a white bread that is different from the coarse black bread traditionally eaten by working people during the week. Two loaves are placed on the table under an embroidered or otherwise decorated cloth. The challah represents the manna given to the Israelites as they wandered in the wilderness; the special cloth symbolizes the "fine layer of dew" that covered the manna (Exodus 16:13-15).

There are many possible explanations for the presence of two loaves on the table. Perhaps the two loaves stand for the two breasts of a woman. Maybe they represent the two portions of manna that the Israelites received on Sabbath eve (Exodus 16:22, 23). In the Bible, challah was the name given to the priests' share of the dough; eventually, the word came to denote the entire loaf. After the destruction of the Second Temple in Jerusalem in 70 C.E.,

Why do Jews clink glasses and say, L' chaim—"To life"? Possibly, the tradition is a remnant of past eras, when people in various cultures believed in the power of lurking demons that attacked at times of rejoicing. The noise of clinking glasses would scare them away. The toast "To life!" also affirms the emphasis on life in Jewish thought.

it became the custom, when baking challah, to separate a symbolic piece of dough in remembrance of the biblical precept of setting apart a portion of dough upon the altar. In addition, the Sabbath challah is often braided, reminiscent of braids added to loaves of bread by German women hundreds of years ago in honor of Berches, a German goddess. This tradition was then adopted by German Jewish women in honor of their own religion.

Every Jewish group has its own special foods for Sabbath, different from those eaten during the week. The Jews of Morocco make a Sabbath meat, rice, and bean dish called *sekhinah*, from the Arabic word for heat; Jews from Eastern Europe cook a similar mixture of meat, potatoes, and beans called *cholent*, from the French word for heat. Both dishes are put in the oven long before Sabbath begins and bake for twenty-four hours, so that the Sabbath day will not be desecrated by someone's lighting a fire to cook; the result is very hot, very brown, and very tasty.

And everyone eats fish—the food symbolic of fertility—prepared ground and boiled and spiced with pepper among Ashkenazi Jews, and spiced and smothered in pungent tomato sauce among Sephardi and Oriental Jews.

The Sabbath would not be complete without the many festive songs sung at home. In the synagogue as well, the Sabbath service includes prayers and song. Some of the most beautiful originated with the mystics of sixteenth-century Safed in Israel: *L'chah - dodi - lik-rat ka-lah, p'nei Shabbat n'ka-b'lah—* "Beloved, come to meet the bride, come to meet the Sabbath." As they sing, many Jews turn to the back of the synagogue, to the west, to receive and welcome the Bride's special protective presence as she arrives for Sabbath.

The Friday night prayers in synagogue and at home conclude with the blessing of children: "May God make you like Ephraim and Manasseh or like Sarah, Rebecca, Rachel, and Leah." An additional blessing, beseeching that all God's children be blessed with peace, is given to all at the end of the synagogue service. Then the Sabbath service is followed by the *oneg Shabbat*, a light repast or dessert, which literally means "Sabbath pleasure" in Hebrew.

Just as Jews welcome the Sabbath with a special ceremony, so they bid it farewell. On Saturday night, after the stars appear, the *havdalah* (separation) ceremony takes place, marking the end of the

In Eastern Europe, young people would go to a certain part of the synagogue where they would play chess with silver pieces crafted especially for these Sabbath afternoons. The people decided that the Hebrew letters in the word Shabbat שבת stand for the first letters of the Hebrew words shach b'ta'anug, *which means "pleasure in chess."*

(sacred) Sabbath and the beginning of a new (profane) week of toil and worry. In the past, this farewell to Sabbath was wrought with fear: when the Sabbath soul was leaving and the stenches of hell returning, when the devils and demons were at work again and there was uncertainty about earning money for the coming week, the Jewish people used this ceremony to insure a good week to come.

The *havdalah* ceremony, which can be found in the prayer book, has many parts: first, the leader—either man or woman—recites a blessing over wine, although the wine is not drunk at this point. Next, a blessing precedes the smelling of spices or flowers, which were once thought to relieve the stench of hell, whose gates reopen at the end of the Sabbath; or perhaps the spices and flowers provide spiritual relief to the Sabbath soul, who is now leaving. A blessing over the light of fire follows. The candle used is either braided, providing more than one wick, or simply extra large. As the blessing is recited, the leader spreads his or her hands toward the candlelight, palms inward, and curls the fingers so that the fingernails point downward; a shadow is cast on the palms, thus reflecting the difference between light and darkness. (In ancient times, people often interpreted these shadows as a means of reading the future.) Then another blessing is recited in praise of God, "who makes distinction between holy and profane." The special *havdalah* cup is passed around; the wine is sipped by all or only the leader. A few drops of wine are poured into a dish, and the candle is extinguished in this wine. The ceremony concludes with songs—one to welcome Elijah the Prophet, in hopes that he will come soon and bring the Messiah, and one to invoke a "good week of joy and peace."

Every part of this ceremony is a legacy from ancient times, when Jews felt it necessary to rid themselves of evil spirits and invoke good ones. Today, Jews are still reluctant to see the departure of the Sabbath, and they use all five senses to prolong its beauty as long as possible. People tell stories, sing happy songs, perform the *havdalah* ceremony, and have a Saturday night feast called *melaveh malkah*, which accompanies the Sabbath Queen (or Bride) on her departure for the coming week.

Besomim Box, Vienna, early 19th century. Judaica Collection of Max Berger, Vienna/Erich Lessing/Art Resource, NY.

THE PIOUS COW

Ancient midrash, translated and retold by Barbara Rush

There was once a certain righteous Jew who owned a cow from which he made a living. Six days of the week he and the cow ploughed together, and when the Sabbath came, he and the cow rested.

Now, the Jew fell upon hard times, and could no longer keep his cow. So he sold his cow to a Gentile, and promised the buyer that the cow was without defect. For six days the Gentile worked the cow without any problem, but when the Sabbath arrived, the cow refused to work. It just sat down and refused to budge. The man beat the cow severely, but the blows did not help. The cow would not do one stitch of work.

The man sent for the Jew. "You tricked me!" he cried. "You told me that the cow was without any defects. For six days it worked, and now it refuses to move. Give me back my money."

The Jew understood what had happened. He went close to the cow, and whispered in its ear: "When you were with me, you observed the Sabbath with me. But now that I have sold you to a Gentile who does not observe the Sabbath, you must work for seven days. Please, for my sake, get up and do your work." And the cow, upon hearing this, arose.

The Gentile was amazed. "Please," he begged, "you must tell me what you said to the cow." And the Jew did.

When the Gentile heard those words, he began to weep: "If this animal who has no wisdom and no understanding, follows the Sabbath, shouldn't I, to whom God has given wisdom and understanding, follow the Sabbath as well?"

At once the man turned to the ways of Heaven and began to study Torah, and became a rabbi. And his name was Rabbi Hanina ben Torta, which means "son of a cow," for, after all, it was a cow that had led him to God.

The Cattle Merchant, Marc Chagall, 1912. Kunstmuseum, Basel/
Scala/Art Resource, NY. © 2000 Artists Rights Society (ARS), New York/ADAGP, Paris.

The Kerchief

By Samuel Joseph Agnon, translated by I. M. Lask, abridged by Barbara Rush

Every year my father of blessed memory used to visit the Lashkowitz fair to do business with the merchants. Lashkowitz is a small town of no more consequence than any of the other small towns in the district, except that once a year merchants gather together there from everywhere and offer their wares for sale in the streets of the town, and whoever needs goods comes and buys them. In earlier times, two or three generations ago, more than a hundred thousand people used to gather together there; and even now, when Lashkowitz is in its decline, they come to it from all over the country. You will not find a single merchant in the whole of Galicia who does not keep a shop in Lashkowitz during the fair.

For us the week in which my father went to the market was just like the week of the Ninth of Ab. During those days there was not a smile to be seen on mother's lips, and the children also refrained from laughing. Mother, may she rest in peace, used to cook light meals with milk and vegetables, and all sorts of things which children do not dislike. If we caused her trouble she would quiet us, and did not rebuke us even for things which deserved a beating. I often used to find her sitting at the window with moist lashes. And why should my mother sit at the window; did she wish to watch the passersby? Why, she, may her memory be blessed, never concerned herself with other people's affairs, and would only half hear the stories her neighbors might tell her; but it was her custom, ever since the first year in which my father had gone to Lashkowitz, to stand at the window and look out....

Whenever father returned from the fair he brought us many gifts. He was very clever, was father, knowing what each of us would want most and bringing it to us. Or maybe the Master of Dreams used to tell father what he showed us in dreams, and he would bring it for us.

There were not many gifts that survived long. As is the way of the valuables of this world, they were not lasting. Yesterday we were playing with them and today they were already thrown away....

But one present which father brought mother remained whole for many years. And even after it was lost it did not vanish from my heart, and I still think of it as though it were yet there.

That day, when father returned from the fair, it was Friday after the noon hour, when the children are freed from school. Those Friday afternoon hours were the best time of the week, because ... even if one does whatever one wants to, nobody objects. Were it not for the noon meal, the world would be like Paradise. But mother had already summoned me to eat and I had no heart to refuse.

Almost before we had begun eating, my little sister put her right hand to her ear and set her ear to the table. "What are you doing?" mother asked her. "I'm trying to listen," she answered. Mother asked, "Daughter, what are you trying to listen to?" Then she began clapping her hands with joy and crying, "Father's coming, father's coming." And in a little while we heard the wheels of a wagon. Very faint at first, then louder and louder. At once we threw our spoons down while they were still half full, left our plates on the table, and ran out to meet father coming back from the fair....

How big father was then! I knew my father was bigger than all the other fathers. All the same I used to think there must be someone taller than he—but now even the chandelier hanging from the ceiling in our house seemed to be lower.

Suddenly father bent down, caught me to him, kissed me and asked me what I had learnt.... Before I could answer, he had caught my brother and sisters, raised them on high and kissed them.

I look about me now to try and find something to which to compare my father when he stood together with his tender children on his return from afar, and I can think of many comparisons, each one finer than the next; yet I can find nothing pleasant enough....

The wagoner entered bringing two trunks, one large and the other neither large nor small but medium; and, that second trunk seemed to have eyes and smile with them....

But we went and undid the straps of the trunk and watched his every movement, while he took one of the keys and examined it, smiling affectionately. The key also smiled at us, that is, gleams of light sparkled on the key and it seemed to be smiling. Finally he pressed the key into the lock, opened the trunk, put his hand inside and felt among his possessions.... There was not a single one among his gifts which we had not longed for all the year round. And that is why I said that the Master of Dreams must have revealed to father what he had shown us in dream.

Sabbath Kiddush Cup, Germany, c. 1738. Judaica Collection of Max Berger, Vienna/Erich Lessing/Art Resource, NY.

The gifts of my father deserve to be praised at length, but who is going to praise things that have vanished and are lost? All the same, one fine gift which my father brought my mother on the day that he returned from the fair, deserves to be mentioned in particular.

It was a silk brocaded kerchief adorned with flowers and blossoms. On the one side it was brown and they were white, while on the other they were brown and it was white. That was the gift which father of blessed memory brought to mother, may she rest in peace.

Mother opened up the kerchief, stroked it with her fingers and peeped at father; he peeped back at her and both of them remained silent. Finally she folded it again, rose, put it in the cupboard and said to father, "Wash your hands and eat." As soon as father sat down to his meal I went out to my friends in the street and showed them the presents I had received, and was busy outside with them until the Sabbath began and I went to pray with father.

How pleasant that Sabbath was when we returned from the synagogue! The skies were full of stars, the houses full of lamps and candles; people were wearing their Sabbath clothes and walking quietly beside father in order not to disturb the Sabbath angels who accompany one home from the synagogue on Sabbath Eves; candles were alight in the house and the table prepared and the fine smell of white bread, and a white table-cloth spread and two Sabbath loaves on it, covered by a small napkin out of respect, so that they should not feel ashamed when the blessing is said first over the wine.

Sabbath Candlesticks, Russia, late 18th century. The Jewish Museum, New York/Art Resource, NY.

Father bowed and entered and said, "A peaceful and blessed Sabbath," and mother answered, "Peaceful and blessed." Father looked at the table and began singing, "Peace be unto you, angels of peace," while mother sat at the table, her prayer book in hand, and the big chandelier with the ten candles, one for each of the Ten Commandments, hanging from the ceiling, gave light. They were answered back by the rest of the candles, one for father, one for mother, one for each of the little ones; and although we were smaller than father and mother, all the same our candles were as big as theirs. Then I looked at mother and saw that her face had changed and her forehead had grown smaller because of the kerchief wound round her head and covering her hair, while her eyes seemed much larger and were shining towards father, who went on singing, "A woman of valor who shall find?"; and the ends of her kerchief which hung down below her chin were quivering very gently, because the Sabbath angels were moving their wings and making a wind. It must have been so, for the windows were closed and where could the wind have come from if not from the wings of the angels? As it says in the Psalms, "He maketh his messengers the winds." I held back my breath in order not to confuse the angels and looked at my mother, may she rest in peace, and wondered at the Sabbath Day, which is given us for an honor and a glory. Suddenly I felt how my cheeks were being patted. I do not know whether the wings of the angels or the corners of the kerchief were caressing me. Happy is he who merits to have good angels hovering over his head, and happy is he whose mother has stroked his head on the Sabbath Eve.

When I awakened from sleep, it was already day. The whole world was full of the Sabbath morning. Father and mother were about to go out, he to his little synagogue, and she to the House of Study of my grandfather, may he rest in peace. Father was wearing a black satin robe and a round shtreimel of sable on his head, and mother wore a black dress and a hat with feathers. In the House of Study of my grandfather, where mother used to pray, they did not spend too much time singing, and so she could return early. When I came back with father from the small synagogue, she was already seated at the table wearing her kerchief, and the table was prepared with wine and brandy and cakes, large and small, round and doubled over. Father entered, said, "A Sabbath of peace and blessing," put his tallith on the bed, sat down at the head of the table, said, "The Lord is my shepherd, I shall not want," blessed the wine, tasted the cake and began, "A Psalm of David." . . .

Mother cut the cake, giving each his or her portion; and the ends of her kerchief accompanied her hands. While doing so, a cherry fell out of the cake and stained her apron; but it did not touch her kerchief, which remained as clean as it had been when father took it out of his trunk.

A woman does not put on a silken kerchief every day or every Sabbath. When a woman stands at the oven what room is there for ornament? Every day is not Sabbath, but on the other hand, there are festivals. . . . On festivals mother used to put on a feather hat and go to the synagogue, and at home she would don her kerchief. But on the New Year

and the Day of Atonement she kept the kerchief on all day long. . . . I used to look at mother on the Day of Atonement, when she wore her kerchief, and her eyes were bright with prayer and fasting. She seemed to me like a presented prayer-book bound in silk.

The rest of the time the kerchief lay folded in the cupboard, and on Sabbaths and festivals mother would take it out. I never saw her washing it, although she was very particular about cleanliness. . . . But for me she would have kept the kerchief all her life long.

What happened was as follows. On the day I became thirteen years old and a member of the congregation, my mother, may she rest in peace, bound her kerchief round my neck. . . . There was not a spot of dirt to be found on the kerchief. But sentence had been passed already on the kerchief, that it was to be lost through me. This kerchief, which I had observed so much and so long, would vanish because of me.

Now I shall pass from one theme to another until I return to my original theme. At that time there came a beggar to our town who was sick with running sores; his hands were swollen, his clothes were rent and tattered, his shoes were cracked, and when he showed himself in the street, the children threw earth and stones at him. And not only the children but even the grownups and householders turned angry faces on him. Once when he went to the market to buy bread or onions, the stall-women drove him away. Not that the stall-women in our town were cruel; indeed, they were tender-hearted. . . . But every beggar has his own luck. When he fled from them and entered the House of Study, the beadle shouted at him and pushed him out. And when on the Sabbath Eve he crept into the House of Study, nobody invited him to come home with them and share the Sabbath meal. God forbid that the sons of our father Abraham do not perform works of charity; but the ministers of Satan used to accompany that beggar and pull a veil over Jewish eyes so that they should not perceive his dire needs. As to where he heard the blessing over wine, and where he ate his three Sabbath meals—if he was not sustained by humankind, he must have been sustained by the Grace of God....

Now I leave the beggar and shall tell only of my mother's kerchief, which she tied round my neck when I grew old enough to perform all the commandments and be counted a member of the congregation. On that day, when I returned from the House of Study to eat the midday meal, I was dressed like a bridegroom and was very happy and pleased with myself because I was now donning tefillin. On the way I found that beggar sitting on a heap of stones, changing the bandages of his sores, his clothes rent and tattered, nothing but a bundle of rags which did not even hide his sores.... The sores on his face seemed like eyes of fire. My heart stopped, my knees began shaking, my eyes grew dim, and everything seemed to be in a whirl. But I took my heart in my hand, nodded to the beggar, wished him peace, and he wished me peace back.

Suddenly my heart began thumping, my ears grew hot and a sweetness such as I had never experienced in all my days took possession of all my limbs; my lips and my tongue were sweet with it, my mouth fell agape, my two eyes were opened and I stared before me as a man who sees in waking what has been shown him in dream.... The sun stopped still in the sky, not a creature was to be seen in the street; but the merciful sun looked down upon the earth and its light shone bright on the sores of the beggar. I began loosening my kerchief to breathe more freely, for tears stood in my throat. Before I could loosen it, my heart began racing with wonder, and the sweetness, which I had already felt, doubled and redoubled. I took off the kerchief and gave it to the beggar. He took it and wound it round his sores. The sun came and stroked my neck.

I looked around. There was not a creature in the market, but a pile of stones lay there and reflected the sun's light. For a little while I stood there without thinking. Then I moved my feet and returned home.

When I reached the house, I walked round it on all four sides. Suddenly I stopped at mother's window, the one from which she used to look out. The place was strange; the sun's light upon it did not dazzle but warmed, and there was perfect rest there.

I stood there awhile, a minute or two minutes or more. Finally I moved from thence and entered the house. When I entered, I found mother sitting in the window as was her way. I greeted her and she returned my greeting. Suddenly I felt that I had not treated her properly; she had had a fine kerchief which she used to bind round her head on Sabbaths and festivals, and I had taken it and given it to a beggar to bind up his feet with. Ere I had ended begging her to forgive me she was gazing at me with love and affection. I gazed back at her, and my heart was filled with the same gladness as I had felt on that Sabbath when my mother had set the kerchief about her head for the first time.

The end of the story of the kerchief of my mother, may she rest in peace.

Friday Evening, Isidor Kaufmann, c. 1920. Gift of Mr. and Mrs. M. R. Schweitzer. The Jewish Museum, New York/Art Resource, NY.

THE TASTE OF THE SABBATH MEAL

Russian folktale, retold by Barbara Rush

On Sabbath eve in the home of Oysher the Jew the mood was festive. Candles were aglow. Blessings were recited. And then, just as the meal was to be served, a knock was heard at the door. There stood the lord who owned the many lands around the village.

"I was walking nearby and was drawn here by the wonderful aroma of your cooking," he said.

"A guest is sent by God," answered Oysher. "By all means, enter and share our Sabbath meal."

And soon, portion after portion was served: spicy fish, steaming soup, crisp chicken ... and each was more delicious than the one before. The guest could not resist licking his fingers—and asked permission to come the next Friday to learn how to cook the Sabbath food. He watched carefully, wrote every detail in a notebook, and sent his servant to buy the ingredients. But when the meal was cooked, it did not taste like the food he had eaten at the home of the Jew.

The lord returned to Oysher's house. "How can this be?" he cried in anger. "I followed your instructions exactly, but my meal was not as tasty as yours."

"My lord," said Oysher, "you did not add a special spice called the Sabbath."

"So what does this Sabbath spice look like?"

"It cannot be seen, my lord."

"And where can I buy it? I'll send my servant at once."

"It cannot be purchased, my lord," answered Oysher with great patience. "On its own, the special Sabbath spice enters the cooking pot of every Jew who keeps and preserves the laws of the Sabbath."

Lighting Sabbath Candles, from Sefer Minhagim, *Amsterdam, 1662. Courtesy of The Library of The Jewish Theological Seminary of America.*

A Closet in the Wall

American immigration tale, retold by Barbara Rush

It was Gittel's first week in America. For two years she had remained behind in Russia, she and the four children, while her husband, Dovid, had saved money—a little each week from his job in the fur shop in New York—to pay for their passage. But now, at last, in December, 1934, the family was together. What joy there was in their tiny apartment! Yes, this Shabbos they would have a great deal to celebrate.

There was so much to learn in this new country. Dovid showed Gittel how to work the gas on the stove, and he showed her the ice box which would be used to cool food in summer. (Who would spend money for ice in the midst of winter?) He took her to the poultry market where she would find the plumpest chicken, and he introduced her to the neighborhood fishman. After all, how could they have Shabbos without fish?

And so, all Friday morning and part of the afternoon, Gittel worked to prepare the Shabbos meal. Just like in Russia, there would be fragrant soup, steaming chicken, gefilte fish, and crispy kugl, a sweet pudding made of noodles. In Russia they may have eaten meagerly the rest of the week, but on Friday night the table was full. And so, now in her new country, Gittel sang as she worked. How proud she was of her Dovid! How proud she was of her American kitchen! And how happy she was at the thought of the coming Sabbath.

When all was ready, Gittel looked for a place to store the Shabbos food, some for tonight and some for tomorrow. As she glanced around her new kitchen, her eyes fell on a closet door on one of the walls. She opened the door—and there in front of her was a small closet with one shelf. A perfect place for her Shabbos food!

But the closet was very dirty. Feh! The stench of rotting food reeked from inside. "No matter," thought Gittel, who had never been lazy. "I'll clean it." And so for several hours she scrubbed with soap and water and a heavy scrub brush until the small closet shone like gold. Then onto the shelf she placed the kugl, the fish, the chicken—all the Sabbath foods.

Soon it was time for Shabbos to begin. The sky outside was dark, and inside the house the candles were lit, standing upright in the cherished candelabra that had belonged to Gittel's grand-mother. Two challahs, the braided Sabbath bread, were placed on the table, and Dovid had bought some Sabbath wine.

After the Sabbath blessings, Gittel went to the kitchen to serve the food. She opened the closet door. But, behold! The food was gone. The shelf was gone. Even the closet was gone. And in its place was a gaping, ugly, pitch black hole. Gittel could not believe her eyes. "I don't understand. I don't understand," she screamed. "How could such a thing have happened?"

Dovid quieted her with a smile upon his face. "My dear Gittel," he said, "God has blessed us by bringing us together for the Sabbath. We can have Shabbos with our challah and our wine."

Gittel realized that Dovid was right, but the children were hungry, and she wondered about her Sabbath meal. What could have happened to it? Yes, America was indeed a very strange place.

Just a few minutes earlier, in his small room in the basement, Beryl the janitor awaited Shabbos with sadness. His wife and children were still in Russia. Every week he saved a little money from his wages as caretaker of the building, but still he did not have the money to pay for their voyage. Perhaps soon. . . .

Sometimes Beryl spent Friday night, erev Shabbos, with other immigrants from his home town in Russia. Sometimes he was invited to the home of a family he met in the synagogue. But this Friday night Beryl would be alone, deep in thought and longing for his wife, Yetta, and their children. How he missed the fragrant Shabbos soup, the steaming chicken, and, most of all, Yetta's crispy kugl!

With these thoughts in mind, Beryl did a quick mental check of the janitorial tasks he needed to complete before the start of Shabbos: the steps of the building had been thoroughly swept, and the boiler oven that makes the heat had been stoked with coal; now there was only one task remaining: the dumb-waiter, that hand-propelled, pulley-driven mini-elevator, built into the walls of the building so that garbage from each apartment could quickly reach the basement below, had to be emptied of carrot peels, soup bones, and other remnants of Sabbath cooking. So Beryl went to the dumbwaiter door and opened it. What he saw made him gasp with surprise. There on the shelf was fragrant soup, steaming chicken, fish, and—WAS IT POSSIBLE?—a crispy kugl, just like in Russia, just like Yetta used to make.

"A miracle!" Beryl cried. "Oy, God remembered me on Shabbos and sent me a miracle." Beryl hurriedly brought the food to his table, before it had a chance to disappear as quickly—and as mysteriously—as it had come.

After reciting the Shabbos blessings, Beryl was about to begin eating when he thought, "You know, Dovid who lives upstairs has just brought his family from Russia—Such an expense!—and maybe they don't have enough money for a Shabbos meal. Why should I have all this food to myself when they have nothing? Surely God blessed me with this fine meal so that I could share it with them."

And so it was that Beryl and Dovid and Gittel and their children soon sat together in front of Beryl's "miracle," which did, indeed, seem to Gittel to be very much like the meal she had just cooked. And Dovid, glowing with happiness, said a special prayer: "Thank you, God, for the good food of Shabbos, and for bringing us together in our new country, where, it seems, closets can change into holes, and holes can change into closets." "Yes, dear God," thought Gittel, "in Your land of America anything can happen."

This story was inspired by a true incident that Gussie Simon related to a collector from the Federal Writers' Project in New York in 1938.

CHALLAHS IN THE ARK

Land of Israel folktale, retold by Rabbi Zalman Schachter-Shalomi

At the beginning of the sixteenth century Jews who had been expelled from Spain tried to settle all over. Some traveled to Salonika in Greece, some to France, some to Germany. One man, whose name was Jacobo, and his wife Esperanza, settled in Sfat, the city where Kabbalah flourished. When he came to Sfat, the only language he spoke was Spanish, so when he went to *shul* and listened to the rabbi's sermons, he didn't really understand everything he heard. One Shabbos the rabbi, who was sixty years old, gave a sermon in which he mentioned that in the Holy Temple God was offered twelve loaves of bread each week before Shabbos. Jacobo didn't understand everything about that sermon, but when he came home he said to 'Speranza, "Next week, Friday morning, I want you to bake twelve loaves of *pan de Dios*, and I am going to bring it to the synagogue. The old rabbi said that God likes to have special bread for Shabbos, and I know that you bake the best challah in the whole country, so next Shabbos I am going to bring Him some of your *challah*." That week 'Speranza baked especially good *challahs*. She kneaded the dough until it was extra smooth, and put all her good intentions into the dough along with the special ingredients. Then, Friday morning, Jacobo wrapped them all up in a nice white tablecloth and took them to *shul*.

When he got to the synagogue, Jacobo looked around to make sure nobody was there, went up to the Holy Ark, kissed the curtain in front of the Ark, and said, "Señor Dios, I bring you twelve *challahs* that my 'Speranza baked. She is really a good baker, and I hope you will like her *challah*. Tomorrow morning when they take out the Sefer Torah, I am going to look inside the Ark, and I expect to see every crumb gone, because my 'Speranza, she really bakes good *challah*." Then he opened the Ark, put the twelve *challahs* inside, arranged them neatly, said "*Bueno apetito*," closed the Ark, kissed the curtain, stepped back seven steps, and walked out of the synagogue very happy that God would have such good *challahs* to eat.

A few minutes later the *shammes* came in with his broom, talking to God. "Seven weeks already with no pay I'm cleaning up the synagogue, and Dear Lord, you know I only want one thing in my life, I just want to be here in your house. I don't want another job, I just want to be the *shammes* here, but Dear Lord, my children are getting so hungry. I know you can do miracles. Please make a miracle for me, I need a miracle so badly. I am going to open up the Holy Ark and I know you will make a miracle. I will find something inside that will help me and my family."

Ark Doors from the Butzian Synagogue in Cracow, Poland, 17th century. Wolfson Museum, Hechal Shlomo, Jerusalem/Erich Lessing/Art Resource, NY.

He walks over, opens up the *Aron Kodesh*, the Holy Ark, and sure enough, there is the miracle. "I knew it! I knew it! The *Ribbono shel Olam* never forsakes anyone." He took the twelve *challahs* and made his way home. When he got home he said, "Easy, easy, not yet. Tonight we will have two *challahs* for the Shabbos table. In the morning, after davening we will have two more *challahs*. For third meal we will have two more *challahs*, and there will be one *challah* for each day of the week. Next week we will see what happens."

Next morning Jacobo came to synagogue, Esperanza went upstairs to the women's section, and they both waited anxiously to see what would happen. When they open up the Ark, will the *challahs* still be there? Or will God have really liked the *challah*, and have cleaned up every crumb? When the rabbi opened the Ark, and reached in to take out the Torah, Jacobo, who had crept up behind the rabbi, peeked in and saw the *challahs* were gone. "Oh, Baruch ha-Shem! Thank God!" He winked up at his wife 'Speranza and went back to his seat.

During the next week Esperanza got the best ingredients she could find. Thursday evening she started making the dough. Friday morning she baked them, fresh and delicious, Jacobo wrapped them up and took them to the synagogue and left them in the *Aron Kodesh* just like the week before. A few minutes later the *shammes* came and picked up his miracle *challahs*. This scene repeated itself every week. The *shammes* found out that if he came too early, or if he hung around the *shul*, no miracle. He learned that he had to rely on God, and not show up until about ten o'clock on Friday, and then he'd find his *challahs* there.

Thirty years passed. One Friday as Jacobo was bringing the *challahs* to the Holy Ark he prayed to God, "Señor Dios, my poor 'Speranza, she is getting arthritis. Her fingers are not so good anymore for kneading the *challahs*. But if you don't like the lumps in the *challahs*, you better fix up my 'Speranza. I hope you enjoy them anyway." He leaves the twelve *challahs*, kisses the hem of the curtain over the Ark, walks back his customary seven backward steps, and—aargh!!—the long bony hand of the old rabbi, now ninety years old, grabs poor frightened Jacobo by the neck.

"What is this that you just did?" yelled the rabbi angrily.

"I brought God His *pan de Dios*, His weekly bread."

"Whatever made you do that?"

"You did, sir. Thirty years ago you gave a sermon about *pan de Dios* in the Holy Temple, and ever since then I've brought God bread."

"Are you crazy? God doesn't eat!"

"Señor Rabino," Jacobo says, "you may be a rabbi, and you may know lots of things better, but He does too eat!"

"What do you mean, 'He does too eat'?"

"For thirty years not a crumb was left in the *Aron Kodesh*."

"Let's hide in the back of the synagogue and see what happens," said the rabbi.

Sure enough, a few minutes later in came the *shammes*, saying, "Dear Lord, I don't know what it is, but something is going wrong with the angels up there. Lately the *challah* has been very lumpy. For thirty years I've been sustained by your angels, so I can't complain, but I just thought you might like to know. Maybe you can ask the angels to bake a little better. Thank you anyways." He goes up to the *Aron Kodesh*, takes out the *challahs*, closes the Ark, walks back a few steps, and—aargh!!—"You terrible man!" the rabbi yells, shaking the poor *shammes*. "On account of you this man has sinned the great sin of anthropomorphism! What do you think you are doing?"

"Listen," the *shammes* explained, "you haven't paid me. This is my *pa'nassa*, my living. Every week God makes a miracle for me."

Soon the *shammes* was crying, because he knew he wouldn't find any more *challahs*. Jacobo was crying because he just wanted to do good. The rabbi began to cry, "How could such a terrible thing come from my good sermon? I never said God eats; it goes against what the Rambam says. God has no body, God doesn't eat. Oy, what terrible people I have in my congregation."

Suddenly Reb Chaim Vital, disciple of the great Kabbalist Isaac Luria, came into the synagogue. "My master, the Ari ha-Kadosh, wants all of you to come to his house." They all went to the Ari's house, and the Ari said to the rabbi, "Go home, make sure your will is in order, because you will die before Shabbos. Thirty years ago your time had come to die. Do you know why you got thirty more years to live? Because since the destruction of the Holy Temple God didn't have as much fun as He has had every Friday morning watching what goes on in your *shul*. He would call all the angels together and they would watch that scene of the man bringing the *challahs*, the *shammes* coming to get them, and God getting all the credit. Since God so enjoyed it, He called the Angel of Death off, and let you live thirty more years. Now that you have spoiled God's fun, go home and get ready, so they can bury your body before Shabbos."

Then the Ari turned to Jacobo and said to him, "Now that you know who has been eating your *challah*, it is going to be a little bit harder, but I want you to believe with perfect faith that if you bring the *challahs* directly to the *shammes*, God will be pleased no less."

ROSH CHODESH

*W*hoever pronounces the benediction over the new moon in its due time
welcomes, as it were, the presence of the Shechinah.

—BABYLONIAN TALMUD: SANH. 42A

Crops are harvested and we celebrate together by the light of the moon. But what if the moon doesn't appear? How can we ensure that it will reappear month after month throughout the year? Perhaps if we bless the moon, it will reappear!

This was the belief of peoples, including the Jews, thousands of years ago. But Jews found a way to celebrate and call forth the appearance of the moon without worshiping it.

Rosh Chodesh—which literally means "head of a month" in Hebrew—is the festival that celebrates the new moon and the coming of each new month. When a Hebrew month has thirty days, Rosh Chodesh is celebrated for two days: the last day of the month and the first day of the new month; when the Hebrew month has only twenty-nine days, Rosh Chodesh lasts for one day and is celebrated on the day after the end of the month.

In biblical times, Rosh Chodesh was marked by the sounding of trumpets and the preparing of special sacrifices, as dictated by Numbers 10:10 and 28:11-15. During Second Temple times, torches were lit on the Temple Mount in Jerusalem to announce the moon. Under Roman occupation, the lighting of such fires was prohibited; thus, following the destruction of the Second Temple in 70 C.E., the festival had changed considerably, characterized by a festive meal for all, no work for men, and no school for children.

But this festival has been a specific time of rest for women, who have always had a special relationship with the moon, possibly because of the connection between the lunar and menstrual cycles: the Hebrew word for moon (*l'vanah*) is feminine. Among mystics, the moon is seen as a symbol of the Shechinah, the feminine aspect of God's presence in the world: as the moon wanes, the Shechinah disappears into exile; then, as the moon waxes again, God's presence on earth is renewed as well.

According to midrash, an interpretation of stories in the Bible, women refused to donate their jewelry to create the golden calf at Sinai (Exodus 32:2); they were thereby rewarded with a holiday celebrated each month throughout the year—and excused from work on Rosh Chodesh. They were also, traditionally, to light candles (possibly a remnant of the ancient Jewish practice of lighting torches at the Temple Mount in Jerusalem) and to enjoy a festive meal.

The Blessing of the Moon, Harry Lieberman, c. 1977. Private collection. Museum of American Folk Art.

The Festival of the New Moon

In the synagogue, on the Sabbath before Rosh Chodesh, the coming of each new moon is announced during the Torah service, at which time congregants beseech God for a new month of blessing and renewal. Candles may be lit, and psalms of praise to God recited. When Rosh Chodesh falls on the Sabbath, the Torah portion is extended to include Numbers 28: 9-15, recounting the sacrifices offered on Rosh Chodesh in the First Temple era.

According to one Talmudic legend (Hulin 60b), the sun and moon were originally of equal size and produced equal light. But the moon was not satisfied and pompously complained to God, asking that one of the two be made smaller. For its haughtiness, God punished the moon, making it smaller than the sun. But in order not to be too harsh, God gave the moon its own realm, called night. The midrash tells us that in the days of the Messiah the moon will be restored to its original size, equal to the sun. Women interpret this prophecy to mean that they will eventually have full equality with men.

Rosh Chodesh ends in a special ceremony, generally performed by Orthodox Jews, called *kiddush l'vanah*, or the hallowing of the new moon. The ceremony is held at the close of the Sabbath nearest to Rosh Chodesh, so that people are still dressed in their best clothes and are in a festive mood. (During the months in which Yom Kippur and Tisha B'Av occur, the ritual is held, instead, at the close of those days.) The ceremony is conducted out of doors, and only if the moon can be seen clearly. A special blessing is recited praising God, Creator of the moon. Readings include selections from Psalms and from Song of Songs. Part of the ritual includes saying *Shalom aleichem*—"Peace unto you"—to three people. The greeting is returned, *Aleichem shalom*—"Unto you, peace." Thus Rosh Chodesh ushers in a new month.

Today Rosh Chodesh remains a sacred time for women. Gathering together, they celebrate the rites of passage (births, marriages) of the members of their group. They mark the day with creativity, weaving in their feelings about the new month, by dancing, lighting candles, and eating special foods; recalling personal memories; reading and creating midrash; hearing accounts of biblical and other women; and singing both secular and religious music. Sometimes men join in the ceremonies as well.

Capturing the Moon in Chelm

Chelm tale, retold by Barbara Rush

In Chelm, the city in Poland inhabited by "wise" folk, the people noticed that the night sky is lit part of the month, and dark for the other part.

"Why can't the moon shine every night?" they wondered. "Then we could take walks every night of the month by the light of the moon."

They soon took their problem to the village elders, the most famous and "wisest" of them all. "We want the moon to shine every night!" they demanded.

The elders, after some deliberation, thought of a plan: "Fill a barrel with water, and leave it open, exposed to the moon's light. As soon as the moon moves into the barrel, cover it quickly. Yes, by so doing [they shook their heads in certainty], you will capture the moon forever." Can you imagine how happy the Chelmites were to hear this plan? They set out at once to carry it out.

A barrel was filled with water, and left open, exposed to the light of the moon. Sure enough, just as they had expected, it wasn't long before the moon moved into the barrel. The Chelmites then sealed the barrel, wrapped it in a heavy sack, and tied it with a heavy rope. Then they sighed in relief. "Surely," they thought, "the moon will not be able to escape now."

For two weeks the Chelmites went about their business, as usual. But then, one night, the sky became dark. "No problem!" said the Chelmites to each other. "We'll open the barrel, take out the moon, and hang it in the sky."

All the townsfolk gathered together in the town square. The eldest of the village elders was given the honor of uncovering the barrel. The people could hardly wait.

But when the barrel was opened, alas! There was no moon! "How can this be? What happened to our moon? How did it escape?" The Chelmites were perplexed, and very disappointed!

The eldest of the village elders put his hand to his forehead, and thought deeply. "The problem," he announced after a few moments of silence, "is that the barrel was not well guarded. If, next month, the moon should once again appear in the barrel, you must seal it quickly and place a guard nearby to keep it from escaping."

"Ah, yes," sighed the Chelmites with relief. "Thanks to the wisdom of our village elders, we now know what to do."

ORIGINS OF ROSH CHODESH

Original midrash by Penina V. Adelman

The festival of Rosh Chodesh was born in the desert where no shadows existed to hide shapes and colors; neither were there many surfaces to muffle sounds. This was a world of no distinctions between land or sky, wind or air; different from Egypt we had just left.

In our wilderness wandering we learned to speak to the heavens and find answers written in the shapes of clouds. The rocks taught us to be patient. The scraggly bushes taught us how to save the rain, embrace the earth. The palm trees clustered together like children around a green pool, showing us how to join them on our knees to drink the blessed water. The desert sustained us all with the same umbilical cord.

Is it any wonder that we who had emerged from the Sea of Reeds together into the wilderness of Sinai all began to live by one rhythm? And is the wonder any greater that the cycles of the moon reverberated in every woman at the same time, in the same way? As soon as the moon was born anew in the sky, each woman began to bleed.

Without saying a word to each other, we women knew it was time to separate ourselves from the men. As if the moon were calling us, we left camp and hiked together to a wadi a half-day's distance. We moved at night over the rocks, surefooted as the lizards. The moon guided us to the place, pulling us with her crescent, a white gleaming magnet in the sky.

When we reached the Wadi of the Moon, we lay on the sand, nestling in the rocks still warm from the daytime sun and fell asleep. That night we all had a similar dream.

One woman told it thus: "We were each bathed very carefully in different ways. The moon bathed us with her light. Our mothers soothed us with the lullabies they had sung to us when we were children. We felt purified with a green fragrance which seemed to emanate from the rocks."

When we awoke, rosemary had sprouted overnight beneath us. We rose as in a spell and embraced each other. Then we began to sing.

Our song seemed to make things grow. There were date palms, figs, grapes, olives appearing all at once and in great abundunce. From a rock a spring trickled forth.

We remained in that desert garden for a week, receiving strength from the earth by seating ourselves in special postures, bathing in the moonlight by night and resting in the shelter of the largest rocks by day.

Soon our bleeding ceased. We watched the moon swell to fullness. It was time to return to our camp.

There we found the men were panicking. They shouted about being abandoned, first by Moses who had climbed the mountain to talk to God and then by us women who had disappeared without a word.

The men feared they would die of thirst. They demanded all our gold ornaments, intending to make a god out of metal. We refused and felt pity for them. They turned from us without asking where we had been. With Aaron reluctantly guiding them, they built an idol. Soon there stood a calf of gold high on a pedestal, beaming foolishly at the mountain. We began to doubt if our week apart in the moonlight had ever happened.

However, in time, with the reappearance of the new moon, we understood our reward: because we had refused to give our ornaments to make an idol, we would be "reborn" each month. The moon would

Miriam's Song of Joy After Crossing the Red Sea, James Jacques Joseph Tissot, 19th century. The Jewish Museum, New York/Art Resource, NY.

teach us about the rhythms of the seasons and the months of the year.

Several women with the best memories became the Keepers of the Months, responsible for remembering which songs were sung, which postures were learned, which stories were told, which ripe fruits were eaten, which type of fragrance the rocks emanated in a particular month so that we could tell our daughters and granddaughters in years to come. We chose the twin sister of the head of each tribe for this task, as it is written, "To each and every [head of the] tribe was born a twin sister...."

This sacred knowledge probably remained hidden over the centuries. As the Jewish people traveled beyond their desert existence, women began to menstruate on different days, each in her own unique relationship to the moon.

The women at Sinai had taken this eventuality into account. They had prayed to the *Shechinah*, Moon of Israel, for guidance. If the sacred knowledge of the months were lost, the *Shechinah* let them know that in a future time when women sought this monthly wisdom once again, it would be rediscovered as easily as moving aside a rock to uncover the fragrant plant beneath. Then the ritual would be reinstated through a community of women who remember, as in a distant dream, how the moon once called to them at Sinai.

We are that community.

May you be inscribed and sealed for a good life.
—Traditional greeting

It is a Sabbath of solemn rest unto you, and
you shall afflict your souls.
—Leviticus 16:31

She Blew the Shofar, Lynn Feldman, 1990. Courtesy of the artist.

Two

Beginning the Year: The Fall

Rosh Hashanah and Yom Kippur

osh Hashanah falls in the month of September, on the first day of the first Hebrew month of the year, called Tishri. It is fitting that the Hebrew words *Rosh Hashanah* literally mean "head of the year."

The Jewish new year is not a day marked on the calendar for frivolity and joyous celebration. Sometimes called the Day of Judgment, Rosh Hashanah is a most serious occasion, the day when God begins to examine and judge the life of every Jew as it has been lived during the past year.

But such a serious time could not occur suddenly, in the midst of the ordinary activity of everyday life. Indeed, an entire month of serious preparation at the end of the year, the Hebrew month of Elul, paves the way for God's judgment. According to the words of a Yiddish proverb, "In the month of Elul even the fish tremble." During Elul, Jews visit the cemetery to commune with those who have played an important role in their lives, asking the deceased to intercede for them in heaven and beseeching God for mercy. Throughout the month Jews study the Bible, sometimes daily, and recite prayers of forgiveness. A special penitential service called Selichot is held at midnight of the last Sabbath before Rosh Hashanah.

After an entire preparatory month comes the first day of the two-day festival of Rosh Hashanah. (Reform Jews celebrate on only one day.) Jews believe that on this day three books are open before God: one for the totally righteous, who are immediately inscribed by God and sealed for the coming year in the Book of Life; one for the totally wicked, who are immediately inscribed in the Book of Death; and a third book that remains open for the majority of people, those who are neither totally wicked nor totally good. These people are held in suspension for ten days until Yom Kippur, which falls on the tenth of the month. During this time, the people must seek

Blowing the Shofar (detail) from Rothschild Miscellany (fol. 137v), Italy, c. 1470. Collection Israel Museum, Jerusalem.

Special foods play an important part in insuring a sweet, fruitful new year. The round challah, studded with sweet raisins, symbolizes the continuous cycles of the year and God's endless sovereignty. Pomegranates, with their many seeds, are believed to bring fruitfulness. Apples, representing the Shechinah, the feminine spirit of God, are dipped in honey to produce a sweet year; for the same reason, mounds of round dough, fried in oil and smothered with honey, are offered. Carrots, cut into small circles resembling pennies, produce good incomes. Also, the Yiddish word for carrots, mehren, means "to increase," as our merits will in the coming year. And, finally, Sephardi Jews eat carrots as they recite, "May it be God's will that the harsh decree on us be torn up." The Hebrew word gezer (carrot) sounds like gazar (Hebrew for "decree").

The Days of Awe

מֹשֶׁה עֶבֶד מִי מִבְּלִי כְבוֹדֶךָ   בְּאָמְרוֹ וּבְיוֹם שִׂמְחַ

וּבְרָאשֵׁי חָדְשֵׁיכֶם וְהָעַ וַהֲבַקַעְתֶּם בַּחֲצֹצְרוֹת עַ

זִבְחֵי שַׁלְמֵיכֶם וְהָיוּ לָכֶם לְזִכָּרוֹן לִפְנֵי אֱלֹהֵיכֶם

אַתָּה שׁוֹמֵעַ בְּקוֹל שׁוֹפָר וּמַאֲזִין בְּרוּעָה וְאֵין

שׁוֹמֵעַ בְּסוֹל תְּרוּעָה עַמּוֹ יִשְׂרָאֵל בְּ

רְיָה   וְסָבִיב   מְטָן   טִיס שׁ

נָסַב   וָלַהַ נָמוֹר   קִישְׁ

יָבִינוּ וִילְכַן

The Hebrew word tashlich *means "you will send." It is the name of an old custom in which, on the after-noon of Rosh Hashanah, people go to a body of free-flowing water and empty their pockets of crumbs, symbolically throwing away their sins of the past year. Based on pagan rites of appeasing the sea god with food, the custom is echoed in the words of the prophet Micah: "You will cast your sins into the depths of the sea."*

the forgiveness of their fellow humans and of God. Rightly called the Days of Awe, these ten days are the time to put one's spiritual house in order.

Each person's fate is determined on Rosh Hashanah and sealed on Yom Kippur. In the synagogue, Jews hear a prayer called *U'ne taneh tokef,* which captures the essence of this first day: "Who shall live and who shall die? Who by fire and who by water?" The prayer is followed by the reminder that repentance, prayer, and righteous acts can avert the harshness of God's decree. Thus, an important message of Rosh Hashanah is that a person's behavior can change predestination. Also, each person is responsible for his or her own actions.

Because they believe that words or deeds can influence the future, the Jewish people have created many ways of ensuring a good year to come. Before and during the Days of Awe, they send to friends and family greeting cards adorned with pictures of a shofar (ram's horn), prayer book, or other symbols of the sea-son that carry the message "May you be inscribed [in the Book of Life]" or "For a good year" or a similar greeting. (Such greetings are given in person as well.) Often, greeting cards depict the Star of David, the national symbol on the flag of Israel. Perhaps cards with this design interweave the holy festival of Rosh Hashanah with the holy space of the Land of Israel.

Yom Kippur in the Synagogue, Antonietta Raphael Mafai, 1931. Private Collection, Rome/Nicolas Sapieha/Art Resource, NY.

The Book of Leviticus (23:24) refers to a sacred occasion, celebrated with loud blasts that was, indeed, called the Day of the Blast of the Shofar, or ram's horn. In the days of the First Temple, this day was not called Rosh Hashanah; nor was it considered part of a new year celebration.

After the Jews were exiled to Babylonia and then returned to Palestine in the fifth century B.C.E., they adopted the name of the month Tishri from its Babylonian counterpart, Tashiru. Hundreds of years later, rabbinic interpretation saw this first day in Tishri as the day of judgment on the anniversary of the creation of the world, and the name Rosh Hashanah ("head of the year") was established. To this day Rosh Hashanah is marked by the memorable blast of the shofar. According to custom, one hundred blasts are to be sounded on each day. The last, long unbroken blast often seems to exhaust the lung capacity of the blower, after which the entire congregation heaves a sigh of relief.

The shofar is blown for many reasons. Above all else, the ram's horn recalls the near sacrifice of Isaac, whose story is read in the synagogue on Rosh Hashanah. When God asked Abraham to sacrifice his son, Isaac, Abraham professed his faith by proceeding to obey God's request. God spared the boy and accepted a ram as sacrifice instead of Isaac.

Biblical interpretation (midrash) tells us that Satan, in several different disguises, unsuccessfully tried to dissuade Abraham from fulfilling God's request to sacrifice his son. The shofar's blast symbolically scares away Satan and other evil spirits, should they decide to influence humans again.

Charity (*tzedakah*) is given throughout the ten days between Rosh Hashanah and Yom Kippur, and special collection boxes for the Days of Awe are available in many communities. Often, donations are made to the synagogue in memory of the dead. The needy are invited to eat, in accordance with the passage in Nehemiah 8:10: "Send portions unto him for whom nothing is prepared."

If you board a public bus in Jerusalem on the days before Yom Kippur, you may hear chickens clucking and see feathers flying—a sign that soup will soon be served, not only in Jerusalem, but all over the world.

This is just part of a meal that, according to the Talmud, God commands Jews to eat on the eve of Yom Kippur, as they anticipate their communion before God. Yom Kippur, called the Day of Atonement, is the holiest and most austere day of the Jewish year.

Yom Kippur was not always a solemn day. In the Bible the day is not mentioned by name. Although the Book of Leviticus declares it "a law for all time," in the era of Solomon's Temple this day, like the Day of the Blast of the Shofar, was largely ignored. Before the days of the Second Temple, both holidays were attached to the harvest festival, Sukkot, and celebrated with great joy: people danced in the vineyards, and young girls donned their finery in hopes of attracting suitors. But in time the rabbis, seeking to solemnize the pre-Sukkot celebration, turned Yom Kippur into the holiest of days, on which the high priest confessed the sins of the people. After the destruction of the Second Temple in 70 C.E., the priest's confession turned into personal confession; the biblical custom of sacrificial rites was replaced by prayer. Several centuries later, in the Talmud tractate Yoma ("The Day"), specific restrictions were listed: no anointing with oil, no bathing, no wearing of leather shoes, among others. Yom Kippur became more like the day Jews now know.

In the home, on the eve of Yom Kippur, candles are lit for the dead as well as the living (*Ner shel Yom Hakipurim* and *Sheh-heh-cheh-ya-nu*); kiddush is recited over wine. On the table, the challah is not braided, as it is for the Sabbath; it may be baked in

Jewish New Year Greeting, Happy Jack, Alaska, 1910. Gift of the Kanofsky Family in memory of Minnie Kanofsky. The Jewish Museum, New York/Art Resource, NY.

the shape of wings to represent the angels the Jews resemble on Yom Kippur (Isaiah 6:2) or in the shape of ladders, which Jews may climb on this day to reach higher spiritual levels. Bland foods are served—no salt, no spice—so as not to induce thirst, because from the sundown following the meal until the next, each adult is required to fast, allowing the body and mind to experience repentance. After the

meal, parents bless their children, as did the Patriarchs at the peak of their holiness. (Words of the blessing may be found in the prayer book.) Then everyone leaves for the synagogue; now the greeting is *Tzom kal*—"May you have an easy fast."

The synagogue is filled to overflowing with men —wearing prayer shawls, soft-sided shoes, and white robes—and women, some wearing prayer shawls and dressed in white as well. All have come to hear the cantor chant the haunting *Kol Nidrei,* sung three times before sundown on Yom Kippur eve. They wear white because it is the color of purity. It is also the color of the shroud— a reminder that death comes to all, so one should not be too proud or vain. *Kol Nidrei,* a plea that originated around the eighth century and was set to music hundreds of years later, asks God to nullify all vows made rashly or unwittingly—not vows made to humans, but those made to one's conscience or to God. (The Sephardi and Ashkenazi versions of *Kol Nidrei* differ slightly in the words and greatly in the melody.)

On Yom Kippur, people come to synagogue to spend the entire day in fasting, prayer, and meditation. Some may even have remained there overnight. This is the final day of judgment, when each person's fate will be sealed in the Book of Life for the coming year. All during the day, the words *G'mar tov* may be heard, as people say to each other, "May you have a good seal." This is the last chance to confess, to atone.

On Yom Kippur Jews are reminded of the partnership between God and humans: God will protect and bless us, and we will be God's people, acting toward one another according to God's standards. Looking into ourselves transforms the way we act. Confession and atonement remove the obstacles that keep us from continuing the covenant with God. As the Torah tells us in Leviticus 16:34, atonement is made not only for the individual but for all Jews.

The day is long; during the service, Jews confess: *Ashamnu*—"we have sinned"—and later in the day they read the biblical story of Jonah (God's mercy and love are universal, and always near). This is also a day of memories: of sacrificial rites in the Holy Temple, of tortured Jewish sages in ancient times, and of Holocaust victims in modern times. The Yizkor prayer is recited in memory of the deceased; candles, lit the night before, burn in their memory.

A modern custom during the Yizkor service, practiced in some Reform synagogues, is to read aloud the list of deaths that occurred in the congregation during the preceding year, followed by the reading of the list of births. This affirms the cycle of life→death→new life and adds a hopeful note to the service.

Jewish New Year Banner, United States, 1942-43. Gift of Mr. Vaxer through Harry G. Friedman. The Jewish Museum, New York/Art Resource, NY.

Toward the end of the service, the Gates of Heaven are almost shut, at which time God's decree will be sealed. The closing prayer of the day, called *Ne'ilah*, comes from the Hebrew word meaning "to lock." The moment is extraordinary: as the sun sets, Jews, weary from their long fast, stand before the opened ark that holds the Torah and pray one last time: "Seal us unto life." Then a loud blast of the shofar resounds throughout the synagogue. Yom Kippur is over.

People rush joyfully out of the synagogue to break their fast with friends and family by enjoying a light meal. A new commandment (mitzvah) must be performed: to drive a nail into the sukkah, the temporary hut about to be built for the coming festival of Sukkot. Thus the end of the Days of Awe leads to new times of joy.

The Most Precious Thing in the World

by Joan Sutton

Once upon a time, God spoke to an angel and said, "For this Rosh Hashana, the New Year, bring me the most precious thing in the world." The angel bowed low to God and then winged her way to earth. Searching everywhere, she visited forests, mountaintops, and soft, green meadows. But although she saw bright butterflies and flowers, nothing seemed quite right. Then, peeking through a window, she saw a mother holding her baby. As she gazed down at her child, the mother's smile was full of love and tenderness. The angel thought, "This mother's smile must be the most precious thing in the world. I will take it to God." Gently, the angel took the mother's smile, but the mother didn't even notice; she had so many smiles left that she would never miss just one! With great excitement, the angel showed the smile to God, who answered, "This is indeed wonderful—the smile of love that a mother gives her child—but it is not the very most precious thing in the world."

So the angel went back to earth and searched again everywhere. One starry night, in the midst of a deep, dark forest, she heard exquisite music; it was the song of a solitary nightingale singing among the trees. The song was so beautiful that the angel folded her wings and listened for many hours. Then she took the song to God. But, upon hearing the music, God answered, "This is indeed very special, but it is still not the most precious thing in the world!"

The angel was getting tired but she knew she could never give up, so again she flew back to earth. This time she arrived in the big city, where she saw crowds of people. They were all in a hurry to get somewhere. They pushed each other as they passed quickly in the streets. They waited impatiently in long lines at banks and supermarkets. They looked nervous and weary. Everywhere there were traffic jams and tired drivers honking angrily.

Standing at one busy intersection was an old man. He was waiting to cross the street, but there were so many cars that he didn't know when to try. People kept rushing past him, never

Tzedakah Box, Tony Berlant, 1994. Skirball Cultural Center, Los Angeles. Museum Collection. Museum commission with funds provided by the Museum Membership, 1994. Photograph by Susan Einstein.

pausing to notice his predicament. The old man felt dizzy and confused. Just then, a young girl came walking up to him. She had noticed him hesitating and looking ill and felt sorry for him. "Excuse me," she said to him shyly, "but may I help you cross the street and walk you home?" Gratefully he gazed into her kind eyes and answered, "Yes, thank you, young lady, I was feeling so tired and weak!" He took her offered arm and walked with her across the street. Slowly and steadily, they made their way to his apartment building, which was nearby.

Now the angel was watching all the time, although the old man and the young girl couldn't see her. The angel was so happy! "This really must be the most precious thing in the world—a kind deed, a mitzvah, a helping hand! It has many names, but it is the same everywhere. If we can help each other, we can have a peaceful world! So I will take the story of this kind deed to God. It must be what I have been looking for all the time!"

God heard the story of the kind deed and answered, "This is indeed important. A mitzvah is one of the most special things in the world—still, it is not quite what I have been waiting for. Go once more, dear angel. You are on the right track, and I feel sure that this time you will find what we seek. Look everywhere— in cities, forests, schools, and homes—but especially look into the hearts of people."

Sighing with disappointment, the angel again winged her way to earth. And she looked in so many places! Still, she could not find the precious thing. "Maybe I should give up! But how could I fail my God? There must be an answer or God would not have asked me to do this." Tired from her ceaseless searching, she sat dejected upon a rock, resting and thinking. As she sat there, she heard something—the sound of someone crying! It was not a little child crying, but a grown man! He was walking through the woods with tears rolling down his cheeks. "Soon the High Holy Days will come, and I am thinking that I was cruel and mean to my dear brother! We had a fight about something unimportant. There were harsh words and now we haven't even spoken to each other in several weeks. Today, this very day, I will go to him and ask him to forgive me. Then I will pray to God to forgive me too, for I am truly sorry that my unthinking anger has caused so much unhappiness." Another tear rolled down the man's cheek.

The angel felt that she had found the answer. Being an angel, she was invisible, so she flew up to the grieving man and gently caught one of the tears that were falling from his eyes. The man thought to himself, "What a soft and fragrant breeze is surrounding me! Suddenly I feel better. Perhaps this is a sign that all will be well!" The angel flew away; she flew away to God. In a small, tiny bottle she held the one tear that she had collected. She held it up to God. And God . . . smiled upon the angel. The radiance of that smile filled the whole world like the sun coming out suddenly from behind dark clouds.

Then God spoke: "My faithful angel, this is indeed the most precious thing in the whole world—the tear of someone who is truly sorry. For it is a tear from the heart, and it will bring peace into the world. The two brothers will forgive each other, and they will enjoy a loving and happy New Year. My dear angel, I bless you for your good work. And may this story be told, so all who hear it can learn from it. L'Shana Tova—a sweet and happy New Year to everyone!"

FIREFLIES IN THE GHETTO

Polish folktale, retold by Barbara Rush

In the days of the Holocaust, the Nazis did not permit the lighting of candles in the Ghetto of Lodz. And why not? First, they wanted to create sorrow for the Jewish people. Second, they were afraid of bombing raids from the air.

In the year 1944, in a narrow room in the Lodz Ghetto, Jews gathered together on the first night of Rosh Hashanah. Several minyans joined in communal prayer. And each heart wept: "Let the sorrows of this past year cease with the coming of the New Year!"

The Gestapo, through the Judenratt, the Jewish council, had declared that not even the smallest candle could be lit. This declaration meant that the Jews of the ghetto were forced to pray in dreary darkness on the first day of Rosh Hashanah.

But when the cantor led the Jews in chanting the traditional prayer, "Blessed Be His Holy Name," scores of fireflies suddenly rushed through the open windows and quickly lit the narrow room. The congregation stood in awe! They did not understand what was happening. But soon they realized that a miracle had taken place: The fireflies, emissaries of God, had been sent to cast light among those Jews who were celebrating the holy day.

Now, when the soldiers of the Gestapo and the Jewish police saw the flickering lights, they thought, "The Jews have chosen to ignore the decree. They have lit their candles before the service." So, at once, a group of Gestapo and Jewish police burst into the sanctuary, shouting commands: "Douse the candles or prepare to be fired upon!" And then a second miracle occurred: The fireflies swarmed the intruders! The Jewish police and the Gestapo were attacked: fireflies destroyed their clothes; fireflies settled on their faces.

Only after this did the S.S. men realize that something extraordinary was taking place before their very eyes. Fredrich Schulza, head of the S.S., began to wonder: "How can fireflies be in Lodz during this time of year?" It seemed to him that this was the beginning of a terrible end. The God of the Chosen People, who had not intervened before, was now making His presence felt.

And so, the head of the S.S. ordered his troops to withdraw and allow the Jews to finish their prayers. Rabbi Mordecai, one of the survivors, related that the miracle of the fireflies lit the hearts and souls of those few who survived the bestial and murderous acts of the Nazis.

Rabbi Mordecai felt that the miracle was not attributed to the fireflies at all but, rather, to Rabbi Yoel, an old peddler in the community of Lodz, who was known, through acts of kindness, to spread his light among ghetto Jews. "Yes," Rabbi Mordecai said, "it was Rabbi Yoel's light that was seen by the people of the ghetto on that Erev Rosh Hashanah—but they were not able to perceive the true light sent by God."

The Holocaust, George Segal, 1982. Museum purchase through funds provided by the Dorot Foundation. The Jewish Museum, New York/ Art Resource, NY. © George Segal/ Licensed by VAGA, New York.

BEFORE

by Penina V. Adelman

A long time ago, before anything had a name, we didn't know that we were man or woman, human or animal, male or female. When the wild reeds bowed their heads in the wind, we bowed our heads too, for it was the same spirit-breath that breathed through us every second, every hour, every day of our lives. At dawn when the brilliant orange squash blossoms opened gently, gently at the first warm kiss of sun, we too opened our eyes and uncurled from sleep, stretching wide, stretching far, rejoicing as every part of our bodies came to life again. And when the rains came forth, loving Earth so much that she grew fruits and berries and nuts to feed us with, we were full of her joy and we loved each other and we grew our own children to eat Earth's joys, her fruits, so that the rains would come again and visit her.

It was before we were called man or woman, even before we could speak one word. In those days we prayed with our entire beings, in the wind, in the sun, in the rain; every second, every day, every hour of our lives; at the rising of the sun and the dark of the moon, at the birth of the son and the death of the grandmother, at the wedding of two lovers, at the buzzing of the Spring. We breathed, we bowed, we laughed, we wept. This was before we called it prayer.

Shofar, Ethiopia, 19th century. Gift of Harry G. Friedman. The Jewish Museum, New York/Art Resource, NY.

The Tale of the Ram

by Rabbi Tsvi Blanchard

Reb Zvi said: "All the hidden things in the universe are hidden together in one small back section of Heaven. There the Messiah waits for the time when he is to come. There also live all of the other great hidden things. There lived the ram, which was sacrificed in place of Isaac. And when you are together in eternity, what you are at your deepest begins to show. And the ram, in a fit of rage at being locked up in a room for so long, gored the Messiah.

"When he came before the Heavenly Court, the Holy One, blessed be He, said: 'Ordinarily, the first time an animal gores it is considered as if it were an accident. But you are a ram with knowledge and wisdom. You are a ram who is like a person, and a person is always considered responsible for the damage that he does. You have gored the Messiah. This shall be your punishment: you shall be put to death, and it shall occur as soon as possible.' With that the ram was transported to the next sacrifice to be made on the face of the earth. He found himself on Mount Moriah, replacing the boy whose father was no longer going to sacrifice him."

Reb Hayim Elya asked: "How badly wounded was the Messiah?" Reb Zvi replied: "So badly that he will come only when his wound is healed."

Ceremonial Plate, Galicia, 19th century. The Jewish Museum, NY/ Photo courtesy of Skirball Cultural Center, Los Angeles.

FROM BAD TO WORSE

Eastern European folktale, retold by Nathan Ausubel

Blowing the Shofar, from *Sefer Minhagim*, Amsterdam, 1723. Courtesy of The Library of The Jewish Theological Seminary of America.

As the rabbi sat deep in thought, a youth came before him and said:

"Rabbi, I want to confess—I'm guilty of a great sin. I failed to say grace one day last month."

"Tsk-tsk!" murmured the Rabbi. "How can any Jew eat without saying grace?"

"How could I say grace, Rabbi, when I hadn't washed my hands?"

"*Oy vey*!" wailed the Rabbi. "How can a Jew swallow a mouthful without first washing his hands?"

"But you see, Rabbi, the food was not kosher."

"Not kosher! How can a Jew eat food that's not kosher?"

"But Rabbi, how in the world could it be kosher; it was in the house of a Gentile?"

"What! You miserable apostate! How could you eat in the house of a Gentile?"

"But Rabbi, no Jew was willing to feed me!"

"That's a wicked lie!" cried the Rabbi. "Who has ever heard of a Jew refusing food to anybody who is hungry?"

"But Rabbi," argued the youth, "it was the Day of Atonement!"

An Arab Shepherd Is Searching for His Goat on Mount Zion

by Yehuda Amichai, translated by Chana Block

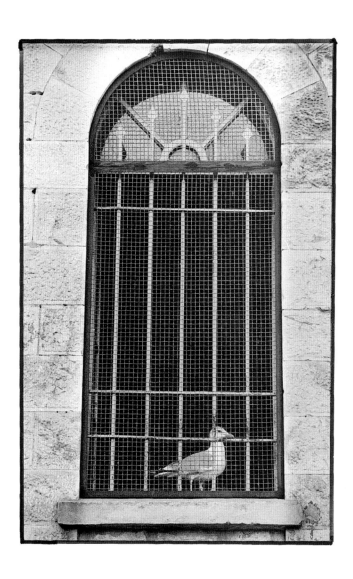

An Arab shepherd is searching for his goat
on Mount Zion
and on the opposite mountain I am searching
for my little boy.
An Arab shepherd and a Jewish father
both in their temporary failure.
Our voices meet
above the Sultan's Pool in the valley
between us.
Neither of us wants
the child or the goat to get caught in the wheels
of the terrible *Had Gadya* machine.

Afterward we found them among the bushes
and our voices came back inside us,
laughing and crying.

Searching for a goat or a son
has always been the beginning
of a new religion in these mountains.

Untitled (Bird in a Gated Window), Aliza
Auerbach, 1992. Courtesy of the artist.

SUKKOT

After the ingathering from your threshing floor and your vat, you shall hold the Feast of Booths for seven days. You shall rejoice in your festival....

—Deuteronomy 16:13, 14

It's late September (or perhaps early in October). There is a bursting in the earth and a fullness of the moon. The harvest is bountiful. Sukkot is truly God's festival, the time to remember God's nurturing. Taking place only a few days after the introspective Days of Awe, the festival is a time to turn outward. Sukkot, which Ashkenazi Jews call Sukkos, may also be called Feast of the Gathering of the Harvest or God's Festival or Time of Our Rejoicing or the Festival of Booths. Beginning on the fifteenth day of Tishri, Sukkot is celebrated for seven days.

In biblical times, Sukkot was the primary festival of the year—even more popular than the spring festival of Pesach—because Sukkot celebrates the gathering of the crops. Farmers, as well as everyone else, flocked to Jerusalem to offer thanks to God in Solomon's Temple, which was, in fact, dedicated on Sukkot (1 Kings 8). Drinking and revelry prevailed among the Jews, just as it did during the harvest festivals of their non-Jewish neighbors.

When the Jews returned to Jerusalem in the fifth century B.C.E., after the exile to Babylonia, the new Temple was the only place to celebrate. Sukkot became a national holiday. Ezra, the priest and scribe who had led the people from Babylonia back to the Land of Israel, read the Torah to the masses. The festival changed from an agricultural celebration to a historical one—a time to remember the Israelites, who, as the Torah tells us, lived in temporary structures (booths) as they wandered in the desert. Because there was always a need for rain in that semiarid climate, part of the celebration also had to include prayers for rain.

Sukkot was the scene of ecstatic celebration: all of Jerusalem was lit by golden candelabra, and the music of cymbals, harps, and flutes filled the air. Women danced with torches held high in their hands. Crowds of men walked by, each one with a *lulav* grasped firmly in his hand. The *lulav*—Hebrew for "palm"—is defined in Leviticus 23:40 as "branches of palm, boughs of lofty trees, and willows of the brook." These branches, plus the "fruit of a goodly tree," were held in the hands, lifted high, and shaken on Sukkot. (The Talmud later identified the branches and fruit as palm, myrtle, willow, and citron—and described how, in Temple times, the bundle of branches was tied together with its own lashings and then covered with strands of gold.) In

Wall Painting in the Sukkah of Fischbach, Germany, early 19th century. Israel Museum, Jerusalem/Erich Lessing/Art Resource, NY.

The Feast of Booths

On Sukkot, the Jews of Alsace in France hang an onion covered with feathers in the sukkah. The Hebrew word for onion is batzal, *which sounds like* batzel, *which means "in the shadow." Alsatian Jews cover the onion with feathers because it reminds them of this passage in the Psalms: "Hide me under the shadow of thy wings." A Talmudic proverb says: "Eat an onion and sit in the shadow"—be satisfied with your lot, and you will have a life of repose. The sukkah—the booth—has been a symbol of humility since biblical times. And so, to the Jews of Alsace, the feathered onion is in keeping with the spirit of the festival.*

the Temple, priests poured water over the altar to remind God to send rain. On the seventh day, the celebrants marched around the altar seven times and beat willow branches into the earth in a symbolic effort to bring forth the needed water.

After the destruction of the Temple in 70 C.E., there was an end to the ceremony of water pouring. Sukkot remained a time to dwell in booths, as the Israelites had done centuries before, to shake the *lulav*, and to pray and read the Torah. For Jews dispersed to the Diaspora, the sukkah, now constructed at home as well as in the synagogue, became the reminder of God's protection. These customs, and this message, have remained with Jews through the centuries.

Today we continue to build the booth, or sukkah, at home and at the synagogue. The sukkah must be located out of doors. Only two walls and part of a third need be constructed, and the walls must be no more than ten feet high. Traditionally covered only with leafy branches, the roof must remain open so that the stars can be seen at night. Today there are many kits for building a sukkah, so it is easy to construct one at home; but the first nail must (symbolically) be driven in at the closing of Yom Kippur.

Because the Talmud associates the sukkah with beauty, the booth should be decorated in an attractive and creative way: with carpets, paper chains, strings of popcorn, fresh fruit, leaves, ears of corn, flowers—even children's drawings. (The fruits and vegetables may not be eaten until the festival is ended.) Sometimes people sprinkle sand on the

floor, as a way of remembering the desert journey of the Israelites, and some Jews from Eastern Europe continue to follow this custom.

When the beautiful sukkah is ready, guests—the poor, as well as friends and family, Jew and non-Jew—are invited inside. From the sixteenth-century mystics comes the custom of inviting seven biblical heroes: Abraham, Isaac, Jacob, Joseph, David, Moses, and Aaron, one on each night. Because all these guests were wanderers, it is fitting that they seek rest in this booth meant to shelter travelers. Among the Jews of India, a Bible is opened each night to a passage about that night's guest and the passage read aloud. Or a person with the same name as the biblical hero may be required to purchase the food eaten in the sukkah that day, as among the Jews of Eastern Europe. Some Jews invite biblical heroines—Sarah, Rebecca, Rachel, and Leah—into the sukkah as well.

During the festival, some Jews regard the sukkah as their permanent home, in accordance with the Bible: "You shall live in booths seven days" (Leviticus 23:42). Others celebrate the festival by eating all their meals in the sukkah. It is a commandment (mitzvah) to eat all the week's meals in the sukkah, unless there is snow or rain. Though not obligated to do so, women usually try to take part, at least through the blessings over Sabbath candles and wine, and a blessing recited whenever a person enters a sukkah. Another blessing—*Baruch Atah Adonai Eloheinu Melech Ha'olam sheh-heh-cheh-ya-nu v'ki-y'manu v' higi-anu la'zman hazeh,* "Praised be God, who has kept us in life, preserved us, and enabled us to reach this season"—is recited on the first night of Sukkot, for it refers both to the first night of the festival and to the first use of the sukkah.

Inside the sukkah, the bundle of *lulav*—the palm, three branches of myrtle, and two of willow—is bound together. These branches, plus the citron (*etrog*)—a large, yellow, sweet-smelling lemon look-alike—make up the four species specified in the Bible. The *etrog*'s stem, called the *pitam*, must be intact; if it is not, the *etrog* is considered defective and may not be used. Also, it is considered best if the skin is bumpy. Beautiful *etrog* boxes, which have been made by Jewish people for centuries, hold the *etrog* when it is not being used.

At home, and in many synagogues, the four species are held in the hand each morning (except on the Sabbath), when each person present shakes the *lulav*, thus expressing joy and gratitude to God. The person shaking the *lulav* stands, grasps the *lulav* in his or her right hand (the spine of the *lulav* must be facing the person), holds the *etrog* in his or her left hand (stem down), and recites the blessing "Praised be God, who instructs us to shake the *lulav*." Then the tip of the *etrog* is moved upward, the hands are held together, and the *lulav* is shaken once in each direction: north, south, east, west, up, down.

On the Sabbath during Sukkot, the well-known passage "To every thing there is a season . . . a time to be born, and a time to die" (Ecclesiastes 3:1, 2) is read. The message of Ecclesiastes and Sukkot is the same: we are here on earth temporarily, so we sit in our booths for a short time only.

In the synagogue on each morning of the festival, hymns that begin with *Ho-sha-nah* ("Save us") are recited, as people circle around the synagogue, just as they once did around the Holy Temple. This circling is perhaps reminiscent of the famous Talmudic legend of Honi the rainmaker, whom the people asked to beseech God for much-needed rain. He drew a circle around himself and prayed to God, refusing to move from the circle until God sent the right amount of rain (Babylonian Talmud: Ta'anit 23a).

The seventh day of Sukkot is called Hoshanah Rabbah (or Great Hoshanah). In the synagogue, the leader wears white, as on Yom Kippur; as some believe, the day marks the end of the period of judgment that begins on Rosh Hashanah. This very serious day never falls on the Sabbath, a day of joy.

On Hoshanah Rabbah, the synagogue is circled, not once but seven times, while the four species are carried and the Hoshanah ("Save us") prayers are recited in full. Then willow branches are tied together and the bundle beaten upon the ground until the leaves fall, perhaps indicating that one's sins from the past year are gone. During the preceding month, Jews have looked inward and turned outward. Now they are ready for the year ahead.

Jews eat special foods on Hoshanah Rabbah: the challah may be round, shaped like a ladder (to Heaven), or in the form of a key (to open the heavenly gates). Also, on this day Jews eat kreplach, a triangular pocket of dough in which meat is concealed, to remind them that God's decree for the coming year is hidden from them.

In Israel, the booths are put on navy boats or on wheels and taken to the sea or into the field, so that sailors and soldiers can share in the joy of sitting in the sukkah.

SHEMINI ATZERET AND SIMCHAT TORAH

O*n the eighth day you shall hold a solemn gathering.*

—NUMBERS 29:35

T*urn it [the Torah] and turn it, for everything is in it. And through it comes clarity of mind.*

—ETHICS OF THE FATHERS 5:26

The biblical passage about Shemini Atzeret reveals that Jews are to tarry with God for one more day after the last day of Sukkot. Some consider Shemini Atzeret (literally, the eighth assembly or gathering) the eighth day of Sukkot, and others observe it as a separate and full festival day. At home, Jews continue to eat in the sukkah, but they do not recite the blessing.

On this day, in the synagogue, Jews beseech God to send rain, because in ancient times, if rain did not fall within a few weeks of Sukkot, crops would wither and the entire nation of Israel would starve.

Upon entering the synagogue, one senses a mood of self-restraint, almost like that on Yom Kippur. The cantor wears a white robe, the ark containing the Torah is opened, and the congregation stands, praying that rain will be sent—for blessing, life, and abundance. One might ask, "Why should Jews recite this prayer outside Israel?" The prayer reminds Jews all over the world that their future is tied to that of Israel.

On Shemini Atzeret, in all but some Reform synagogues, the Yizkor service is held in memory of the deceased. Perhaps the outpouring of tears will entreat God to send rain, or remembering the deceased may cause them to intervene in heaven on behalf of the living, after which the much-needed rain will fall.

Simchat Torah (literally, joy in the Torah), a day of rich and beautiful symbols, marks the completion of a year of Torah readings and the beginning of a new cycle. For many Jews, it is an additional (ninth) day of Sukkot, or, as established more than a thousand years ago, it is the second day of Shemini Atzeret. Jews in Israel, and Reform and Reconstructionist Jews in the Diaspora, celebrate Shemini Atzeret and Simchat Torah on the same day.

Since the Middle Ages, the custom on Simchat Torah has been to circle the synagogue seven times as the congregants hold the Torah scrolls and dance and sing in its honor; more than eight hundred liturgical songs of praise (called *piyyutim* in Hebrew) have been written in various Jewish languages—Yiddish, Ladino, Hebrew, and Judeo-Arabic—to be recited on this day. All the scrolls are removed from the ark and adorned with gold or silver crowns, or, in some communities, with fine silk or wreaths of flowers. After the scrolls have been removed, a lit candle may be placed inside the ark, so that the Holy Ark is never without light.

Still Life with Jewish Objects, Issachar Ryback, 1925. Collection Israel Museum, Jerusalem. Photograph © Israel Museum/Yorah Lehmann.

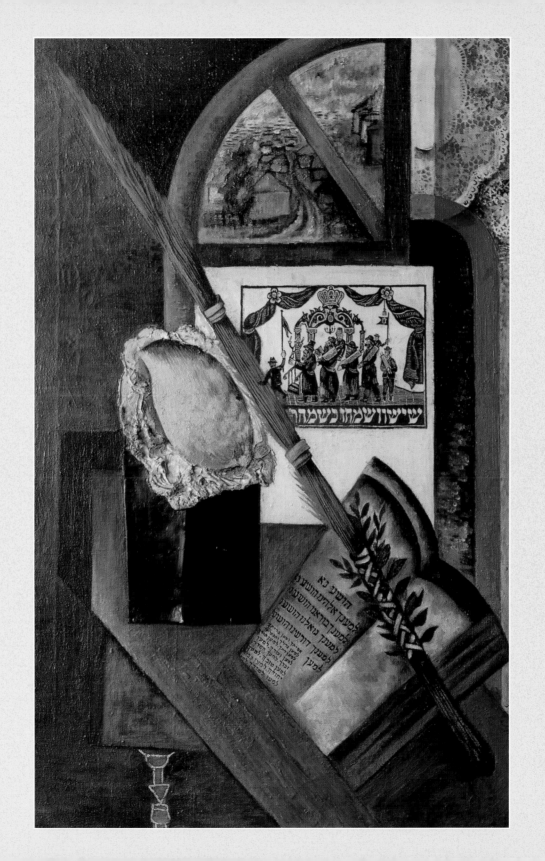

Then, after the seven circlings (called seven *hakafot*), every Torah scroll but one is returned. In a mystical imitation of the wedding service, the remaining Torah is treated like a bride, showered with song, dance, and joy; a deserving person, or an actual groom, is designated the Groom of the Torah. This tradition is based on the custom of calling bridegrooms to the Torah on the Sabbath after seven days of marriage, and being chosen is a coveted honor. The "groom" reads the three final verses of the Torah, followed by the opening verses of Genesis. Sometimes two grooms are chosen (one called the Groom of the Law; the other, the Groom of Genesis). The first reads the closing verses of the Torah; the second reads the opening verses. So it is that the reading of the Torah never ends.

The analogy between Simchat Torah and a wedding is further underscored in Israel with massive dancing processions to the Western (Wailing) Wall, led by men carrying Torah scrolls under a canopy, just as the bride and groom are carried at a wedding. The joy of this procession symbolizes the delight of continued study of the Torah.

The joyous holiday of Simchat Torah would not be complete without special foods. Cabbage is featured, because the Hebrew word for cabbage (*k'ruv*) also means "cherub." By eating cabbage, Jews are reminded of the cherubim on the Ark of the Covenant, which the Children of Israel built according to instructions in Exodus 25: 18-22 and carried with them through their desert wanderings.

Just as it is a festive, joyful, noisy day for adults, Simchat Torah is a very special time for children as well. In Germany, during the Middle Ages, children too young to attend synagogue were showered with candy at home. Even today, children old enough to attend synagogue feel the excitement of being called up to the Torah, under the canopy of a large prayer shawl or tallit, and blessed, as Jacob blessed his grandchildren (Genesis 48). How special it is to receive the gift of a prayer book—or mini-Torah—and to be treated to sweets and honey! What a wonderful connection the child receives to the joy and sweetness of Torah study!

In Israel, and in the Diaspora as well, children may march with an Israeli flag (the symbol of Jewish nationalism) topped by an apple, which is likened to the sweet Torah. The cored apple may be used as a holder for a lit candle, the symbol of the Torah's light.

Simchat Torah from *Sefer Minhagim*, Amsterdam, 1662.
Courtesy of The Library of The Jewish Theological Society of America.

THE CLEVER JUDGMENT

Tunisian folktale, retold by Barbara Rush

In a certain house in the city of Tunis there lived two families, one Jewish; the other, Muslim. The Jew lived on the second floor, and the Muslim lived on the first. The Days of Awe passed, the festival of Sukkot arrived, and the Jew built a sukkah on his porch and covered it with branches of palm and olive.

When the Muslim saw the beautiful sukkah, he was very jealous. So, what did he do? On the first day of the festival he went to the police station and told a lie: "The Jew brought a lot of branches to his porch and built a building there. When the winds blow, the dirt and twigs fly into my house."

Succot from
Sefer Minhagim,
Amsterdam, 1661.
Courtesy of The
Library of The
Jewish Theological
Society of America.

At the police station, the Muslim captain ordered one of his officers to bring the Jew at once. And when the Jew arrived, the captain asked him, "Tell me the truth, what did you build on your porch?"

The Jew answered humbly, "I didn't do anything, sir. I did not build or break anything. We Jews have an old custom of erecting a sukkah out-of-doors on our holiday, and since I have no other place to put it, I made use of my porch."

The police captain, a clever man, thought for a while. "I rule that you have built an illegal structure," he declared. "I set aside eight days' time, beginning from today, in which you must tear down the building that you have erected. And, if you don't destroy it within that time, I will fine you harshly and send you to jail."

The Muslim returned home, happy that in eight days' time the Jew would have to take down his sukkah.

The Jew returned home, happy, satisfied, and full of thanks. He and his family rejoiced during their holiday. And the fact that they had to take their sukkah apart after eight days did not lessen their joy even a tiny bit.

That was a clever judgment, wasn't it?

A Tale of
Reb Nahum Chernobler—and a Tikkun

Chasidic folktale, retold by Eve Penner Ilsen

*When a tale is told about a known Chasidic rabbi, we do not have the right to simply change
the story to suit our tastes and times. So, following the original story, an alternate ending–
a* tikkun *(repair)–answers my question, "And what if it had happened differently?"*

Reb Nahum of Chernobyl and his family lived in
the direst poverty. While he was intensely
engaged in a holy life of prayer and learning, ministering to the needs of his community, it fell to his
wife, the Rebbetzin Sarah, to do everything else.
She cared for the house, the cleaning and shopping
and cooking, the washing and mending. She bore
and raised the children, keeping them safe and as
healthy as she could and teaching them the ways of
menschlichkeit, of becoming good human beings.
And what meager living sustained them, she made.
Often, the pillows, candlesticks, and other house-
hold items had to be pawned just to put food on the
table for Shabbos. Often, these items stayed at the
pawnshop longer than expected. Sometimes they
never came back home at all.

Reb Nahum's poverty was voluntary. When his
hasidim would offer gifts to make his life easier and
more comfortable, the rebbe would refuse. He did
not want to be distracted from essentials and
become attached to the material things of this world;
and he had a positive dislike for owning money. He
preferred to attach himself to things he considered
of permanent value: *Torah* and *mitzvos*; and for
these he was willing to make sacrifices. For instance,
the joy he felt in fulfilling the *mitzvah* of putting on
tefillin in the morning was enhanced by a very special pair of *tefillin* that he owned. They were the only

items of any real monetary value in the whole house.
The small scrolls had been written by a very holy
scribe, each letter fashioned with intense *kavannah*
(inner purpose) in a unique script. Reb Nahum treasured these *tefillin* and held them in high regard.
When he bound them to himself, he felt he could fly
in his prayers far above his physical surroundings.

Other pious Jews knew about the *tefillin* as
well, and several of the better-off householders had
asked to buy them. In fact, one man had offered
Reb Nahum four hundred rubles! That was enough
to marry off a daughter, from the expense of a
matchmaker and a respectable dowry through the
wedding celebration with musicians, new clothes
for the bride and groom, and enough to feed all the
poor of the town plus the honored guests, with
even a little left over. This was an enormous sum.
And all this while, Rebbetzin Sarah continued
struggling to make ends meet. When times were so
hard that she did not know where the next meal
would come from, when the children were hungry
and there was nothing left to pawn, she would
approach her husband and plead with him to sell
the *tefillin*. "My husband," she would say, "if you
sell your *tefillin* and replace them with a more ordinary pair—no small expense—still, what would
remain, if I managed carefully, could free us from
worry for a long time. After all, isn't the *meaning* of

the verses written in the *tefillin* what is really important? And isn't that the same in every pair of *tefillin*? And isn't it the *kavannah*, the intent, that counts most when you *daven* your own?"

But Reb Nahum wouldn't hear of it. "Don't worry," he told her. "The Holy One will help us." And somehow, they continued to squeak by from day to day, from Shabbos to Shabbos, from season to season, from festival to festival.

One autumn, it was almost the eve of Succos and Reb Nahum had still not found an *esrog* (citron) to make the blessing in the *succah*. *Esrogim* were always imported with cost and difficulty from the warm countries to the East, since they would not grow in the colder climates of Russia. This year there was scarcely an *esrog* to be found in all of Chernobyl. As the last afternoon leading to Succos deepened, Reb Nahum was beginning to wonder seriously how he would be able to fulfill the *mitzvah* of blessing the *lulav* and the *esrog* as commanded for the festival, when he had a stroke of extraordinary good luck. He came upon a traveler rushing through Chernobyl on his way home for Succos; and among his other possessions, he was carrying—an *esrog*! Without thinking for one moment of cost, Reb Nahum begged him to sell him the *esrog*. At first the traveler was unwilling to part with it at any price. But, when faced with Reb

Etrog Container, Germany, 19th century. Skirball Cultural Center, Los Angeles. Museum Collection. Photograph by John Reed Forsman.

Nahum's entreaties, the traveler told himself that if the *esrog* was so important to the rebbe, the money was equally important to his family, and he owed it to them to consider selling the *esrog*—but only for a stiff price: 400 rubles. It was exactly the sum that Reb Nahum had been offered for his *tefillin*.

Reb Nahum stood in thought: on the one hand, he wouldn't need his *tefillin* for the next eight days, since on *Succos* one isn't obligated to wear them. And on the other hand, this was the only time in the whole year that he could fulfill the *mitzvah* of blessing the *esrog*. So he quickly came to a decision. He asked the traveler to wait a short time while he ran to complete a business transaction and return with the money. He ran home, took his *tefillin*, and rushed to the house of the buyer who had offered him four hundred rubles before, and who now happily paid the high price and considered himself lucky. Reb Nahum took possession of the rare *esrog*, and he sent the traveler off with the four hundred rubles and a blessing. He wrapped the *esrog* in its protective coverings and put it carefully in its box. Once home, he put it in a special place so that nothing would damage the delicate fruit and spoil it, for the fruit had to be whole and perfect in order to be used for the blessing in the *succah*.

As Rebbetzin Sarah was making the last preparations for greeting the holiday—making the food and

Succot Decoration, France, 18th century. Musée Alsacien, Strasbourg/Erich Lessing/Art Resource, NY.

the house and the *succah* as neat and festive as possible on next to no money—she caught a faint whiff of the sweet scent of *esrog*. She knew it wasn't possible; even if an *esrog* were to be found in Chernobyl, they hadn't the money to buy it. So she smiled to herself, thinking that the very thought of Succos was strong enough to draw down the vivid memory of the fragrance. Then she caught sight of the box, unmistakable in its safe place. Such a box, such a fragrance—it had to be an *esrog*. She didn't believe her eyes.

Just then, Reb Nahum entered the room.

"My husband, that couldn't be—an *esrog*?"

"Yes!" Seeing her look of disbelief, he took down the box, opened it, and unwrapped the fruit to show her.

"How wonderful! But—how did you ever manage to buy it?" she asked.

And he told her what he had done.

One Traditional Ending

Something in her snapped, after all those years of hardship and privation.

"The *tefillin*?" she gasped. "Your precious *tefillin*, which could have supported the whole family for so long, which I have been begging you for years to sell and you refused—you *sold* them today, to buy from a passing traveler an *esrog* that we will use for only seven days?"

The rebbetzin was beside herself with fury.

She seized the *esrog* and bit off the *pitom* end.

Now the *esrog* could not be used for the festival.

Reb Nahum was silent for a long moment. Then he said: "My precious *tefillin* are gone. And now, the *esrog* is lost to me. Satan would now like me to lose one last thing to make his victory complete: my temper. *And that I will not do.*" And Reb Nahum left the room.

One Possible Tikkun

Something in her snapped, after all those years of hardship and privation.

The rebbetzin was beside herself with fury.

She seized the *esrog*, bit off the *pitom* end, and burst into a high, keening wail.

Reb Nahum stood frozen in shock. He had, by a near miracle, managed to acquire an *esrog* in time for Succos, the only time in the whole year that he would have the opportunity to perform this *mitzvah*. Now they couldn't use it. And his wife was crying as if her heart would break.

"Sarah, Sarah, what is it? Why did you do this? Please, talk to me!" He stood by helplessly while she rocked herself to and fro, convulsed by sobs, almost retching. He had never seen her so distraught. A long time passed before she could breathe easily again, and it was longer before she could speak.

"My husband," she whispered, "for years you have been *davennen*, learning, teaching, and caring for the needs of the community." He looked at her, head to one side, puzzled. "For those same years," she said, "I have barely been able to snatch a moment to pray at length, not on the run, let alone to learn a little. Because I have spent every waking moment of every hour keeping worry from you, making it possible for you to do what you do, and eking a life out for ourselves and our children." She was trembling.

"And it's barely a life. Sometimes our sons can hardly keep their minds on their learning because of the rumblings of their empty bellies. We shiver and our noses run for over half the year because we can't afford more wood for heat." Her voice, soft and intense, began to gain strength. "Our daughter is almost of an age to marry, and all of her few rags of clothing are threadbare. When it comes time for her wedding, will she even have a dowry?"

She continued: "When I asked you to sell your *tefillin*, it was not for the sake of luxuries, but in order to buy bare necessities. Did you think that I would ask you to part with your treasured *tefillin* for the sake of a frivolity? Each time I asked, and you told me God would provide. God *did* provide—something. Then you would tell me not to worry: didn't I see, God had provided. But I *live* in worry: in what form will God's help come? Of course our sustenance comes from Him; but every evening, it is *me* that you and the children ask for dinner. It is my task to see that it gets from God to the table. I use all my heart and all my strength trying to patch it together so we can survive. It is my job to persuade the shopkeepers to wait just a little longer until we can pay our bills. Whatever comes, I am the one who counts each *kopek* [penny] and makes it stretch to last."

Rebbetzin Sarah's voice lowered to just above a whisper. "My husband, do you really think it is right that we all pay such a high price for your attachment to poverty?"

Reb Nahum sat in shocked silence. His eyes filled.

For the first time, Rebbetzin Sarah had found her voice.

And now, for the first time, Reb Nahum found his ears: he heard her deeply.

He moved closer to her, and they looked deep into each other's eyes.

Cradling the ruined *esrog* between them, the couple stood and cried together, the salt of their tears sweetened by the fragrance of the fruit.

And we are told that the joy of Succos had never been sweeter in their house than in that year.

WHEN THE RAINS RETURN

Syrian folktale, adapted by Cherie Karo Schwartz

In this retelling of a tale called "A Jar of Tears," the male character Rachamim (which means "compassion") has become the more earth-centered female Rachama. And, in this version, the tale continues with the fate of the jar and the appearance of the miraculous tree.

It was a time of drought. There was no rain. There was no dew upon the grass. There was no water in the streams or the rivers. The earth was parched. The people were parched, and their skin had begun to wither; and the animals withered, too. Every day, those who were young and still strong enough were sent to walk miles to the muddy river far away to bring back small pails of water so the people could live.

The heavens would not open. It would not rain. There was no water, save that shed by the people as tears.

The Rabbi called his entire congregation together, and together they prayed. They prayed fervently. The Rabbi reminded them to think of anything they had done wrong as individuals or as a community in the last year, and to pray from the depths of their hearts, but still there was no rain.

They prayed all night and into the next day, sick with thirst, but still there was no rain.

In the midst of their prayers, the Rabbi thought he heard a voice ask, "Where is Rachamah?" He opened his eyes, looked around the tiny congregation, and there was no Rachamah.

The Wealth of Job from Rothschild Miscellany (fol. 65), Italy, c. 1470. Collection Israel Museum, Jerusalem.

Rachamah was an old, quiet woman who lived in a small hut on the edge of the town. She kept to herself, lived by herself, and people rarely saw her. "Where is Rachamah?" the Rabbi asked out loud. "Where is Rachamah?" A whisper passed through the congregation: "Where is Rachamah? And, why would the Rabbi ask?" The entire congregation stopped their prayers to listen. Everyone knew the answer: she wasn't there! She hardly ever came to the synagogue, and after years of asking, they all had let her be by herself.

The Rabbi left the *bima*, right in the middle of the prayers, walked through the congregation, and went out the door. The minutes passed, and then, through the open door came the Rabbi…with Rachamah.

The Rabbi and Rachamah went to the front of the congregation, and Rachamah turned to face the people. In her hands was a small clay jar. She held it in front of her, and, as the people watched, her lips began to move as if in prayer. She held the small clay jar up before her, and she spoke in a small whisper. As she continued to speak, her voice gained in power, until all could hear her prayer.

"Dear God, our land, our animals, our children are dying. The people grieve. I have been grieving for years for so many reasons, but I do not let it show. When things have been too hard for me to bear, I cry, but I do not let the tears just dry and go away. I gather the tears of my grief in this little jar. They are all here. Dear God, we are all starving. The earth is dying and so are we all. This is not right. If you will not restore the rain, then I will take this jar of my tears and smash it on the ground—smash it and let all the tears run out."

Rachamah stopped and she stood still and silent. The whole congregation watched, waiting—but for what? A sound began, far off, and no one could be sure what it was. Then there was a low rumble, soft at first, but gradually it became louder and closer. Suddenly, lightning split the sky, thunder shook the synagogue . . . and the rains came. The rain began as quietly as Rachamah's whisper, and then it grew loud enough to drown out all of the voices in the congregation and all of the pain in the people's hearts.

Rachamah just stood before the congregation. The people were whispering, talking, shouting, praying with joy. They opened the door of the synagogue and watched as the rain came down to replenish the earth.

And the rain, now steady and gentle, came in abundance.

The people sat and looked in wonder at Rachamah. They looked at the small clay jar. What a miracle! They reached for it.

But Rachamah, holding her small clay jar, moved away, walked out of the synagogue, into the blessed rain, and back to her own small house.

The next day, the people went to visit her, many for the first time, and asked to see the small clay jar. "I have returned it to the earth," was all she would say. And no one ever saw it again.

The rains came in their season, the people and the animals thrived, and the earth was restored. Months passed, and one day some children noticed a small tree growing next to the synagogue and wondered where it came from.

Years passed, and the sapling turned into a strong and beautiful tree, and red fragrant blossoms appeared on the branches. Then the flowers fell, and tiny green fruits began to grow. They grew bigger and rounder and then turned deep red. The branches of the tree had grown to touch the synagogue as though to protect it. The pomegranate tree was beautiful, and it lent its beauty to the synagogue. The children came and picked the pomegranates and they said that they were the sweetest they had ever eaten.

People came from all around to see the beautiful tree and to taste the sweet juice of its fruit.

And some people say that they know how such a tree came to grow on that spot. They say they know the source of the tree. They say that they remember the story of Rachamah and the rain, and they know the connection. For inside every pomegranate, there are hundreds of seeds. And each one is shaped like a small, wet tear.

Thanks to God Who Gave Us the Toyre

Polish folktale, retold by Barbara Rush

Torah Crown, Galicia, c. 1770. Gift of Harry G. Friedman. The Jewish Museum, New York/Art Resource/NY.

Once, on Simchas Toyre*, when the synagogue overflowed with men, women, and children, all in a happy state of mind, jubilant, singing, and joyous, Reb Yehuda suddenly appeared amidst the congregation. He was an ignorant Jew who often disobeyed the laws of the Toyre. But now, during the circling, he excelled in his dancing and devotion. His joy was greater than that of the pious Jews, those who were learned and most respected.

One of those present asked, "Reb Yehuda, all year long you are far from the Toyre and its commandments. Why do you now feel such great joy in the holy Toyre?" "I have sufficient reason for being joyous on the holiday of Simchas Toyre," answered Reb Yehuda. "I am happy, first, that it was the Holy One, blessed be He, who gave us the Toyre. Because, had the Kaiser given us the Toyre, we would have to observe it 100 percent. I am happy, too, that He didn't give it to the other nations of the world. And why? Because had the Holy One, blessed be He, given the Toyre to the other nations, they would be wreaking vengeance against us and forcing us to observe all its commandments. So you see," the man continued, "I am happy that the Holy One, blessed be He, gave the Toyre to us Jews—for with Jews it is always possible to compromise."

* *The pronunciation in Eastern Europe.*

These days should be kept with gladness and praise at
their due season, year after year, for eight days, from the
twenty-fifth day of the month of Kislev.

—First Book of the Maccabees 4:59

WE KINDLE
THESE LIGHTS
ON ACCOUNT OF
THE MIRACLES,
THE DELIVERANCES
AND THE WONDERS
WHICH THOU DIDST WORK
FOR OUR FATHERS
BY MEANS OF THY HOLY PRIESTS.
DURING ALL THE EIGHT DAYS OF CHANUKAH
THESE LIGHTS ARE SACRED,

NEITHER IS IT
PERMITTED US
TO MAKE ANY
PROFANE USE
OF THEM;
BUT WE ARE ONLY
TO LOOK AT THEM,
IN ORDER THAT WE MAY GIVE
THANKS UNTO THY NAME
FOR THY MIRACLES, THY DELIVERANCES
AND THY WONDERS.

Ben Shahn

CHANUKAH

In December, on the twenty-fifth day of the Hebrew month of Kislev, the day is short, the night long and dark. Jews participate in a festival during which, originally, they implored the return of sunlight. The ancient celebration, similar to that of their surrounding neighbors, evolved into Chanukah, the eight-day festival of lights, with its distinctly Jewish messages of nationalism and spirituality. At certain times in history, the nationalistic aspect has been more important; at other times, the religious aspect has dominated.

Chanukah celebrates the victory of a small, ill-equipped band of Jews over the large, well-equipped army of Antiochus Epiphanes, the Hellenistic king of the Syrian branch of Alexander's empire, in 165 B.C.E. During this reign, biblically ordained practices such as circumcision and Sabbath observance were forbidden upon threat of death, and pagan rituals were instituted in the Holy Temple. Then, in 168 B.C.E., in the small town of Modin near Jerusalem, Mattathias, a member of the priestly class and the Hasmonean family, defied the order of Antiochus to bow down to the Greek gods. Mattathias escaped to caves in the mountains, where

for three years his son Judah (called the Maccabee) led a small group of farmers in a three-year guerrilla-type revolt against the Greeks.

On the twenty-fifth day of Kislev, Judah and his band emerged victorious. They then rededicated the altar of the Temple (the word *Chanukah* means "rededication" in Hebrew), marched with their *lulavs*, traditionally held on Sukkot, and gave offerings to God. The eight-day festival celebrated the military victory of the Maccabees; this eight-day period was perpetuated in Israel as a religious festival from that time. Some people think that because the Maccabee army had no time to celebrate Sukkot during the war, the eight-day celebration was their Sukkot: seven days of Sukkot plus the extra day of Shemini Atzeret.

The story of the Chanukah festival is found not in the Bible but in the later writings of the Apocrypha. The First and Second Book of the Maccabees, written independently of each other within a hundred years of the Maccabee victory, describe the rededication of the altar in the Holy Temple but not the tradition of kindling eight lights. However, as every Jewish schoolchild knows, the

In many Sephardi and Eastern communities, boys born during the month of Kislev are often named Nissim, the Hebrew word for miracles. A fitting name for a Chanukah baby!

The Festival of Lights

festival of Chanukah celebrates the miracle of a small jar of oil, sufficient for one night, that burned for eight nights in the Holy Temple. Where did this story come from? Why did the emphasis of the festival change?

The Scroll of Antiochus, an early rabbinical account of the Chanukah story, contains the narrative of the miracle in the Temple. It was written about 100 C.E., some thirty years following the destruction of the Second Temple. A story about the rededication of the Temple altar was no longer needed, but the masses of Jewish people under the oppressive rule of Rome, which had replaced sixteen decades of Greek rule, needed hope. Therefore, the story of the jar of oil lasting eight days instead of one was born, and a new spiritual message was proclaimed: "There's no reason to despair. God's miracles will occur again." The festival of Chanukah provided an excellent opportunity for spreading the word. Chanukah became a tribute to God, not to the Maccabees or their Hasmonean descendants. And the kindling of lights, which had arisen as a spontaneous custom, was sanctioned by the rabbis and included in the Talmud as religious law.

Especially in the twentieth century, with the rise of Zionism and the State of Israel, Chanukah has again come to symbolize the military victory of the Maccabees. So now we light the candles to celebrate two great events: one, a victory of the few against the many; the other, a miracle of a little oil giving much light. On a personal level, Chanukah has become a time to reflect, "How can I bring light out of darkness in my own life?"

Almost all of the Chanukah celebration takes place at home, and because it has few religious restrictions, the festival is easy to observe. Kindling the lights in a special Chanukah candelabrum is the first and foremost observance, prescribed by Jewish (Talmudic) law. But the material, size, and decoration of the candelabrum (correctly called a *chanukiah* and commonly called a menorah) is not prescribed by law and is left to the individual imagination. Throughout history and around the world, these candelabra have been made of ceramic, glass, metal, and wood; they have been painted, carved, and embossed; and they have ranged in height from a few inches to the height of a person. The common denominator of every *chanukiah* is that it has eight lights, one for each night that, according to legend, the oil burned in the Holy Temple.

The Talmud specifies that lights be placed in the doorway of the house to proclaim God's miracle to everyone. Women (who traditionally light festival candles) and men are obligated to light the menorah because, indeed, men took part in the miracle. The candles, lit after sunset, are to be tall enough to burn for at least half an hour; during this time, no reading or other work is to be done. Once they are lit, the lights are not to be extinguished. In most Jewish homes today, people kindle colorful candles made of wax, but one can also use wicks and clean olive oil, as did the Maccabees in ancient days.

An extra candle, called the *shammash* (Hebrew) or *shammos* (Yiddish), is used to light the other candles and is usually placed beside or higher than the others. Most menorahs have one *shammash*, but sometimes there's an additional one.

If you ride up and down the streets of a Jewish neighborhood during Chanukah, you will probably see electric menorahs in many windows, an

The various spellings of the eight-day festival in English–Khanukah, Hanukkah, Chanukah–all

have eight letters. Perhaps this is a way to emphasize the eight days of the miracle.

outgrowth of the religious decree to proclaim the miracle to everyone. If you display a window menorah, reverse it so that the candles—as seen from the street—are in the correct position.

Watch the excitement on children's faces as they light the candles, especially if there is a *chanukiah* for each family member! The candles are lit as follows: first, the candle for the *shammash* is put in its place. Then the correct number of candles (one for the first night, two for the second night, and so on) are placed at the right side of the menorah. The *shammash* is lit and then used to light the other candles from left to right. As the candles are lit, the first blessing is recited or sung: *Ner shel Chanukah*— Praised be God, who commands us to light "the light of Chanukah." Then the blessing *She - a'sah nissim l'avoteinu - ba'yamim hahem ba'zman hazeh*—Praised be God, "who made miracles for our fathers, in their days, in this time." On the first night, this is followed by *Sheh-heh-cheh-ya-nu*—Praised be God, "who has kept us in life," preserved us, and enabled us to reach this season.

After the blessings, in a spirit of joy, everyone sings songs such as "Rock of Ages," "Who Can Retell?" or *Al Hanissim* ("On the Blessings").

And then more sounds of joy follow—the paper wrappings crinkling, the *oohs* and *aahs* as children receive their presents—not only on one night but on eight! Gift-giving has become the custom among Jews in Christian countries, where Christmas gifts are exchanged. Coins (*gelt* in Yiddish), which children were given on Chanukah in Eastern Europe to sweeten the study of Torah, are still bestowed upon children today.

Chanukah is a time for parties—and eating! From Jewish kitchens around the world wafts the smell of oil—because the common denominator of many Chanukah foods is that they are fried in oil: potato pancakes, called *latkes* in Yiddish, are served with sour cream or applesauce among Ashkenazi Jews; vegetable pancakes, called *levivot* in Hebrew, are prepared by Sephardi and Eastern Jews; heart-shaped pancakes are the custom among Libyan Jews (note that the Hebrew word *lev*, meaning "heart," is part of the word *levivot*); deep-fried sweets dipped in honey are traditional in Greece and Iran; and doughnuts, fried and dipped in sugar, are the most popular in Israel.

Chanukah is a favorite holiday among women because of the brave and heroic deeds of women in the Chanukah story. The first was a mother, later named Hannah, whose story is written in the Second Book of the Maccabees. She let her seven sons be tortured to death rather than bow down to the idol of a strange god. In the popular thinking of the time, this type of death was considered to be for the good of the entire community.

In Israel, where the Chanukah miracle took place, a torch is lit in Modin and carried,

relay style, to Jerusalem. Thousands of schoolchildren, each holding a lit candle,

gather at the Western Wall in Jerusalem, where a huge chanukiah is lit.

For a few thousand years, especially during the Middle Ages, Jewish people liked to play arithmetical word games to challenge the mind. One such game, called *gematria*, involved affixing a numerical equivalent to each letter of the Hebrew alphabet: 1 = א, 2 = ב, etc., with some letters having numerical values of multiples of ten or one hundred. Equivalencies were created from the numerical values of words.

During Chanukah Jews play a game with a spinning top called a *dreidel* in Yiddish and *s'vivon* in Hebrew. Each of the four sides of the top is inscribed with one of these letters: ש, ה, ג, נ, which begin the Hebrew words *Nes*, *Gadol*, *Hayah*, *Sham*, meaning: "A great miracle happened there." This refers to the miracle of the small flask of oil lasting for eight nights in the Temple. Thus, by spinning the top, Jews are remembering the past.

At the same time, the spinning of the top is also a way of divining the future. According to *gematria*, the numerical equivalent of the Hebrew letters ש, ה, ג, נ is 158. This same number is assigned to the word משיח, or *mashiach*, the Hebrew word for Messiah. By spinning the top, the player calls for the Messiah to come, for the world to be restored to peace.

If you live in Israel, the letters on your *s'vivon* will be: פ, ה, ג, נ, standing for "A great miracle happened here." The numerical equivalent of these four letters is 138, the same as the numerical equivalent of the Hebrew word *lekach*, part of the biblical verse from Proverbs: *Lekach tov natati lachem* – "I give you a good doctrine." This biblical connection lends the spinning top a sense of the sacred.

Rules for playing the dreidel game are that each player receives an equal pile of pennies, candies, or nuts. Each puts one into the center. Then each player, in turn, spins the dreidel. The letter it falls on determines what that person may receive or do:

Nun נ means nothing is yours;
Gimmel ג means take all;
Hei ה means half is yours;
Shin ש or *Pei* פ means put in another.

The aim is to win everything from the other players. Before each turn, each player puts one coin into the center.

Dreidl, Michael Berkowicz and Bonnie Srolovit, 1993. Purchased with funds given by the Judaica Acquisitions Fund, 1993. The Jewish Museum, New York/Art Resource, NY.

A GEMATRIA CHART

ת	ש	ר	ק	צ	פ	ע	ס	נ	מ	ל	כ	י	ט	ח	ז	ו	ה	ד	ג	ב	א
400	300	200	100	90	80	70	60	50	40	30	20	10	9	8	7	6	5	4	3	2	1

Judith with the Head of Holofernes from the *Rothschild Miscellany* (fol. 217), Italy, c. 1470.
Collection of Israel Museum, Jerusalem. Photograph © Israel Museum/David Harris.

The second notable woman, also called Hannah, was the sister of Judah the Maccabee and his four brothers. Her story is told in first- and second-century writings. At that time, every new bride was sent to spend her wedding night in the bed of the local (non-Jewish) governor. But on her bridal night, the sister of the Maccabees undid her robes and stood naked in front of the masses rather than sleep with the non-Jewish governor. Ashamed and appalled, her brothers wanted to slay her, but she cried out, "Why do you not defend a daughter of Israel?" (as did the brothers of Dina when she was raped [Genesis 34]). After this outcry, Hannah's brothers rose to her defense. Thus, according to legend, began the revolt of the Maccabees—not for religious reasons, but in defense of a woman's honor.

The third heroine is the brave Judith, whose story is related in the apocryphal Book of Judith. In order to save her people, she seduced Holofernes, the general of the enemy Assyrian army, fed him salty cheese, quenched his thirst with wine until he fell asleep, and killed him. Jewish women from Ethiopia to Russia have used Judith as a model for their own tales about how they bravely saved their own Jewish communities in times of danger, and the figure of Judith is depicted on Chanukah candelabra in many countries. And, to remember Judith, many Jews eat cheese on the festival.

In some countries, women were traditionally given a holiday from work during Chanukah. And on Rosh Chodesh Kislev, the first day of the month in which Chanukah falls, men in many communities presented gifts to their wives and daughters.

Chanukah is a joyous, fun-filled holiday that memorializes an important victory and miracle in ancient Jewish history.

A Chanukah Miracle

Eastern European folktale, retold by Barbara Rush

As the month of Kislev approached, the Jews of the village remembered Alexsis the Gentile, who lived across the swamp. Every year, on the nights of Chanukah, he would light the candles and make a feast for the village Jews. A special pan was kept for this celebration and fresh oil purchased each year from a village Jew.

By evening the small hut was full of people: men, women, sons, and daughters—all had come. Dressed in their holiday clothes, they had bravely piled into their sleighs to make their way across the frozen swamp.

Now seated on the benches that had been brought from far and near for this special evening, they were greeted by Alexsis, who, with his beard combed and hair washed for the occasion, heartily welcomed his Jewish guests. Flasks of vodka stood on the table. Sophie, Alexsis's plumpish wife, brought forth several bowls, each heaped high with crispy latkes.

And then Alexsis melted down the bottom of a candle to better fix it to the window sill. Everyone waited for the candle to be lit, but Alexsis was not yet ready. Instead, he turned to the village people and quietly told them the story that they had heard many times before, each year on a Chanukah night:

"That year the winter came early. It was bitter cold, and I, with permission to gather dead branches of the trees, went to the forest and loaded the wood onto my wagon. It was so cold that the work was very hard, and I did not realize that evening was approaching. I urged my horse to go more quickly, as I heard the howling of hungry wolves behind me. So fiercely did I beat my horse that his hair stood up from fear of the whip, and instead of running on the road to the house, he ran between the trees and lost his way. The growling of the wolves grew nearer, nearer. The horse jerked loose from his bridle, and I, out of great fear, jumped from the wagon and began to run and cry, 'Help! Help me!' For how long I ran I do not know. The forest was dark and full of frightening sounds.

"Then, suddenly, I saw the faint flickering light of a candle. Following it, I came to the hut of the Jew, Reb Pinchas, whose job it was to watch the forest. After hearing my urgent story, he left with me for the place where I had last seen my horse. Taking his hunting rifle

Chanukah, from *Sefer Minhagim*, Amsterdam, 1728. Courtesy of The Library of The Jewish Theological Seminary of America.

from his shoulder, he began to shoot— thus keeping the wolves at a distance, so that we could make our way back to the wagon. When we reached the place, we found the horse lying down but still alive, the teeth marks of the wolves freshly ground into his feet. Reb Pinchas continued to shoot as I helped the horse get up and put him in his bridle. Then we made our way back to his home.

"Once inside the warmth and comfort of the little hut, I said to the ranger, 'You have saved my life! How can I repay you?' Reb Pinchas looked into my eyes. 'I need no payment,' he answered. 'To know that I have helped a lost traveler is reward enough.' I remained at the feet of this good man, and as I looked around, my gaze fell upon the flickering lights that had showed the path of safety only moments before. 'Tonight is the night of Chanukah for the Jews,' he explained. 'It is our custom to light candles to remember the miracles that happened to our fathers in days of old.' I remained pensive for but a moment—and then I spoke. 'From this time on, I, too, will light a candle on the nights of this holiday. The candles shall be a reminder to me of the miracle that happened here on this Chanukah night!'"

Every Jew sat in silence as Alexsis came to the end of his tale. Although they knew the story by heart, they listened as though they were hearing it for the very first time.

Then Alexsis lit the candles. Joyfully the Jews of the village sang "Ma-oz-Tsur," and Alexsis sang and danced with them.

The Fourth Candle
by Mara

Rachel's father walked over to the dining room cabinet. He opened it up, took out the Menorah, and began to walk toward the kitchen. "Where are you going?" Rachel asked. She was eleven years old. Her father looked at her mother as if to say, "You explain it to her."

"Rachel dear," her mother began, "we're going to light the candles in the kitchen this year."

"Why?" asked Rachel.

"Well dear," her mother began, "we don't live in New York City anymore, and there aren't any other Jewish people in this town. It would be strange and even odd to light a Menorah out front. So we're going to light the candles in the kitchen. Okay?" Her mother smiled, a little too cheerily, and hoped her daughter would understand.

"But Mom ... Dad ... I thought you always said it was important to light the candles out front. You said it was important to remember the courage and strength of the Maccabees. That it was a message. You said it was like a light in the darkness ... or something like that. I . . . I thought you said it was important to light them out front," Rachel blurted out in anger and confusion.

Her parents looked at each other and then finally her mother said, "Well, perhaps we could light the first night's candles out front." And with that Rachel took the Menorah and walked toward the front room. She did not hear her mother say to her father, "It's only two candles. Maybe people will think it's a Christmas decoration."

Rachel walked to the front window and parted the curtains. She placed the Menorah in the middle of the window. "Oh," she thought to herself, "it is going to be so beautiful. And surely someone in my class will see it and say something to me." Or at least she hoped that would happen.

It just seemed that ever since she began attending this new school a few months ago, none of the kids had any time for her. They all had other friends and family. No one seemed interested in getting to know Rachel. There were even a few kids who lived on her block. One of them was Brad Brown. His father was the fire chief. Sometimes Rachel would try to start a conversation as they walked home, but he would always look at her strangely and then walk across the street.

Well, she was certain that someone would see her Menorah and say something to her the next day. And so, with that certainty, she lit the shamash and then the first night's candle. Her parents stood behind her with uneasy expressions.

She went to school the next day and, at the very end of the day, someone did say something to her. It was Brad Brown, the boy from across the street.

"Hi," Brad said gruffly. "My dad wants to know where you got those candles."

"Oh, you saw my Menorah? Did you like it?" Rachel was so excited. "Actually, we had to get them

Statue of Liberty Chanukah Lamp, Manfred Anson, 1985. Skirball Cultural Center, Los Angeles. Museum Collection. Museum purchase with Project Americana funds, provided by Peachy and Mark Levy. Photograph by Susan Einstein.

about twenty miles out of town because there aren't any other Jewish families in this town. But you saw my Menorah? Did you like it?"

"Um," Brad stammered, "you know, my father is the fire chief. Well, he needs to know if they're fireproof." Then, as suddenly as he had appeared, he turned and walked away, leaving Rachel alone. For the first time in her life, Rachel began to feel a knot in the pit of her stomach.

She walked home with that knot and told her parents what had happened. Her parents asked if she still wanted to light the candles. "Yes, yes I do!" she responded without hesitation.

And so that night she lit the second night's candles, and then she went to school the next day. No one said anything. She lit the third night's candles and went to school the next day, and still no one said anything. At least if someone would say it was inappropriate or that she was not allowed to—but *no one* said *anything*. And that knot in her stomach kept growing and growing. Finally, she became so uncomfortable that she decided to light the fourth night's candles out front, but no more after that.

That night she walked to the front window and again parted the curtains. She lit the shamash, and then the four candles for that night. She thought to herself how beautiful the Menorah looked. Then the phone rang. Her father answered it and called to her, "Rachel, it's the Brown boy from across the street."

Rachel walked over and took the phone from her father. "Hello?" she said. In an abrupt and harsh voice, Brad said, "My father wants to know if it's important that you put it out in *full view?*"

Rachel was startled but blurted out, "Yes, yes, it is important. There's a message being conveyed. A message about the courage and strength of the Maccabees. There's a . . ." But Brad cut in and said, "The message has been delivered." There was a click and the phone went dead.

Rachel's legs began to shake beneath her as she slowly sat down and hung up the phone. She quietly told her parents what had happened. And then in a resigned voice she said, "Mom, Dad, I guess you were right. I am going to take the Menorah out of the window now." She slowly stood up and walked out of the kitchen to the front room.

Silently, she looked at the Menorah in the front window for the last time. Two of the candles had already burned down, but two were still burning brightly. It was so beautiful. She noticed how the candles were being reflected in the window directly in front of it. That brought her attention to the outside and she could see some of her neighbors had already put up their Christmas lights.

Then she saw something that made her smile. Her Menorah was being reflected in the window across the street. And it reminded her of what it was like in New York when there were Menorahs on all the streets . . . in all the windows. "It was nice then," she thought sadly.

And then she noticed something else. Her Menorah had two candles burning, but the Menorah across the street had . . . three candles burning. "Mom! Dad!" she called out.

Her parents rushed into the room, and the three of them stood huddled together as they silently watched Brad Brown and his parents light the fourth night's candle. Rachel's mother held her family close and said, "Yes, Rachel, it is like a light in the darkness."

TU B'SHEVAT

It is forbidden to live in a town which has no garden or greenery.

—BABYLONIAN TALMUD: KIDD. 4:12

The Talmudic legend (Ta 'anit 23a) of Honi the sage reveals that by planting trees Jews express thanks to those who planted before them and show their concern for those who will come after them. Tu B'Shevat, which takes place on the fifteenth day of the month of Shevat, usually in January or February, was once a celebration of trees; but it is now a festival of people who plant, cultivate the products of, and care about trees. Jews are especially appreciative of trees and plants, both in the Diaspora and in the Land of Israel, to which they are connected on this day.

The name of the festival, Tu B'Shevat, according to the numerical equivalencies of the Hebrew letters, literally means the fifteenth day of the month of Shevat: 9 = ט, 6 = ו, 15 = טו. Among some Jewish groups, it was also customary to connect the Land of Israel and the number fifteen by singing Psalms 120-134, as did the Levites while they ascended the fifteen steps to the inner court of the Temple.

There is a historic connection between the Jewish celebration of Tu B'Shevat and the date on which it takes place. The biblical passage of Deuteronomy 14:22 decrees that one tenth of a farmer's income be given to support the priesthood and the poor; this sum included a ten-percent tax on fruit. The sages established the date

Tu B'Shevat Celebration, Michal Meron, 1995. Courtesy The Studio in Old Jaffa, Israel.

Honi the sage once saw an aged man planting a carob tree. "Why are you planting?" Honi asked. "Don't you know that it takes seventy years for this tree to bear fruit? Surely you will die before then!"

"No matter," answered the aged man. "As my grandfather planted for me, so will I plant for my grandchildren."

Honi went on his way, and as he walked he grew tired, and so he lay down and fell asleep. But this was no ordinary nap. Honi slept for seventy years! And when he awoke, he came to the place where the old man had planted the tree. There he saw a young man picking the fruit of the tree and feeding it to his child. "Who planted this tree?" Honi asked. "My grandfather," the young man replied.

Then Honi knew he had slept for many years. He understood the wisdom of the old man's words, and of planting trees for others.

The New Year of the Trees

Plate for *Tu B'Shevat*, Austria, 19th century. Israel Museum, Jerusalem/Erich Lessing/Art Resource, NY.

of the fifteenth of Shevat, the time when fruit begins to flower, as the end of a year's fruit crop and the beginning of a new one; thus, the "new year" of the trees was a fiscal one. After the destruction of the Second Temple in 70 C.E., the tithing was continued to help Torah scholars and students in the Diaspora.

By Talmudic times, the rabbis regarded the new year as one in which the trees themselves were personified, based on the story of Jotham in Judges 9, in which this happens. At this time of year, the rabbis thought, trees drink the rain that has fallen all winter and then begin a new life. And on this day, the Rosh Hashanah of the trees, God judges them.

The sixteenth-century mystics of Safed in Israel saw the image of the *Sephirot* (emanations of God) as a tree. Tu B'Shevat then became a Rosh Hashanah for God, a day on which God renews the flow of life to the universe. The mystics saw the eating of fruit, dedicated with the proper blessing, as a symbol of the renewal of this flow of life. In an effort to make the festival holy, these mystics developed a Tu B'Shevat seder, at which four cups

of wine were drunk and four fruits or other plants were eaten.

Several centuries later, in Europe, it became customary to remember the Land of Israel by eating fruits grown there. To overcome the difficulty of bringing fruit in winter from Palestine to Europe in time for Tu B'Shevat, people began their journeys from Palestine to Europe on the previous Sukkot or Chanukah. The fruits they carried included olives, dates, grapes, figs, and pomegranates—which the Torah says are part of the goodness of the land—and carob, which sustained the second-century sage bar Yochai in his flight from the Romans. (He is honored on Lag B'Omer.)

Today, because there is no biblical, Talmudic, or other religious authorization of Tu B'Shevat, there are no specific practices. Tu B'Shevat has become the time to plant vineyards and trees, as Jews are commanded in the Torah; this act is crucial to restoring the land, especially in Israel. In the Diaspora, planting trees in Israel may be done via the Jewish National Fund, which was established in the early 1900s for this purpose. Or people may plant trees in their own community.

In Israel and the Diaspora, Tu B'Shevat is also a time for sharing and eating fruits, especially those that come from Israel: figs, dates, carob, and nuts, like almonds (the almond tree is the first to bloom in Israel). Fruits are blessed with the appropriate words: *Borei pri hagafen* (Praised be God, Creator of the fruit of the vine) or *Borei pri ha'etz* (Creator of the fruit of the tree). The *Sheh-heh-cheh-ya-nu* blessing is recited over fruit being eaten for the first time that year.

And on Tu B'Shevat, people donate money to the poor, or to Mazon, an international organization whose name means "food" in Hebrew. Mazon collects and distributes money to feed the hungry throughout the world.

Jewish customs for Tu B'Shevat vary: North African Jews traditionally wore fruits as pendants; in Persian communities, children lowered empty baskets down the chimney—to be returned full of fruit. In Eastern and Central Europe, children brought fruit to school to share. At home, these fruits were eaten on ceramic Tu B'Shevat plates beautifully painted with fruits. Today, in the United States, schoolchildren are given boxes or bags of fruit to share at home.

The Tu B'Shevat seder has been continued, particularly by Sephardi Jews, and guides for creating a Tu B'Shevat haggadah are available from synagogue Judaica shops and Judaica bookstores. At these seders, the table is usually set with a handsome cloth, candles, and fine dishes, to parallel the Passover seder. Customs, such as the four cups of wine and four fruits introduced by the sixteenth-century mystics, continue as part of the Tu B'Shevat seders. In Israel and the Diaspora, there are parties and singing. "The almond tree is blooming; here the sun is shining" are the words of a favorite children's song for Tu B'Shevat.

Also on Tu B'Shevat, Jews pray for a sweet *etrog* (citron) next Sukkot (the fruit is an integral part of the Sukkot celebration), so that from it they may make fruit preserves for the next Tu B'Shevat. The sacredness of each festival is tied to the next, as the cycles of the year continue.

On Tu B'Shevat, as on other days, Jews act in partnership with God. During this festival, they are reminded that they are God's representatives, God's caretakers on earth. Because they appreciate God's bounty, they recognize their responsibility for the earth's well-being. Tu B'Shevat has become a time to learn about the environment and to think of new ways to preserve it. It is a time for Jews to ponder, "What can we do this year to become *shomrei adamah* [keepers of the earth]? How can we protect the ecology and the environment?" The Torah tells us: "When in your war against a city. . . . you must not destroy its trees, wielding the ax against them" (Deuteronomy 20:19). If we protect the trees of our enemies in time of war, should we not protect the earth, air, and water when there is no war?

Money is sometimes donated in the amount of 91 dollars or 91 cents, because according to the gematria, in which a numerical equivalent is affixed to each letter of the Hebrew alphabet, 91 is the numerical equivalent of ilan, *the Hebrew word for tree.*

A Tu B'Shevat Miracle

Greek folktale, retold by Barbara Rush

This tale, one of the few about Tu B'Shevat, recounts how trees bless and kiss each other on their new year, just as humans do on theirs. Legends tell about the Sambatyon River, beyond which live the Ten Lost Tribes. During the week the river throws up sand or stones, and so it is impossible to cross it. On Sabbath, when the river rests, it is equally impossible to cross because a person may not desecrate the Sabbath by traveling. So the Lost Tribes continue to remain in exile. The folk imagination envisioned that the tribes were made up of tall, strong, brave men called the Children of Moshe (Moses), who live a full Jewish life on the other side of the river and who can be called upon to help fellow Jews in times of need. During the Middle Ages, when Jewish communities were being expelled and destroyed, many a traveler set out to find these legendary Jews

One evening the king disguised himself, as was his custom, and, with his vizier, went to walk in the outskirts of the city. Passing through an alley, he heard sounds of singing coming from a small Jewish school, where young children studied aloud, watched over by their teacher. The king tarried awhile and listened to the words of the songs, uttered in a language unknown to him and then translated into the vernacular. His ear caught the verse from Deuteronomy: "How can it be that one pursues a thousand, and two cause ten thousand to flee?"

Greatly astonished by these words, the king was determined to find an answer to the question. He entered the school and said to the teacher, "I just heard children's voices singing this verse: 'How can it be that one pursues a thousand, and two cause ten thousand to flee?' Tell me, what man could possibly have such strength?"

"You must, sir, take your question to the Chief Rabbi himself. He will answer your question." And so, the very next day the king commanded one of his officers to bring the Chief Rabbi before him.

"Honored Rabbi," began the king, "yesterday at dusk I passed your school, where little children were studying aloud, and my ears heard them sing the verse: 'How can it be that one pursues a thousand, and two cause ten thousand to flee?' Indeed, if there is such a man, I must meet him."

"Most respected King," answered the rabbi, "our holy Torah is the Torah of truth. Yes, there are men, one of whom can pursue a thousand, and two cause ten thousand to flee. Children of Moshe is what these men are called, and all of them are tall, heroic, and brave, but the land in which they live is very distant."

"If you speak truthfully," said the king, "let one of these men come before me. I grant you thirty-one days to fulfill my command. But if you fail, I will order the death of every Jew in my kingdom."

The rabbi left with a heavy heart. In so short a time, could they find a man from the Children of Moshe and bring him here? Great fear fell upon the Jews. They dressed in sackcloth and put ashes on their heads, as one does in times of mourning. They declared a fast of thirty days and thirty nights, gathered in the synagogue, and prayed, "Please, dear God, rush to our aid and cancel the decree." An announcement was made to the community: "Whoever is willing to risk his life by going as our representative to the land of the Children of Moshe, let him make himself known!"

Tu B'Shevat, from Sefer Minhagim, Amsterdam, 1723. Courtesy of The Library of The Jewish Theological Seminary of America.

Palestine Exhibition Poster (detail), 14th Zionist Congress, Vienna, 1925. Central Zionist Archives, Jerusalem.

Now, among those who prayed was a certain scholar who ached in his heart for the sorrow of his people. "I will go!" he cried out. So it was that early the next morning the rabbi explained the route to the land of the Children of Moshe and gave the messenger a letter for their rabbi, urging quick aid for the Jewish flock that now was in such trouble.

The Jew took provisions for the road, mounted his donkey, and set out. Each day he rode on his way, and each night he climbed a tree and slept upon its branches, so as to protect himself from beasts of prey. Thus the Jew traveled for many days, until he reached a dense forest. He continued on his path, coming at last to a wide river that divided the forest in half. Being tired, he dismounted his donkey, tied it with a

rope to the branch of a tree, refreshed himself with a light meal, and climbed into one of the trees.

Now, this particular night was the night of Tu B'Shevat, the New Year of the Trees, when it is the custom of trees to kiss one another and wish each other a happy new year. And that is how the tree in which the Jew was sleeping went to kiss his fellow trees across the river, taking his new burden with him. And, as the tree in which he lay kissed another, the Jew rolled from the first tree into the second, and then from the second into the third, and so on, all night long. Being in sound sleep, the Jew did not sense his movement.

In the morning he awoke, descended from the tree, and looked around to find his donkey—but it was gone. He soon discovered that his feet were standing at a stream, and that not far away were two tall maidens, filling their pitchers with water. When they spied him, the young girls stared at him in wonder. As he neared, one of them extended her hand. "Who are you? Where do you come from and what is your wish?"

The Jew's heart beat with excitement, for he understood that his feet had come to rest in the land of the Children of Moshe. He answered the girl's questions and told the two of his mission. The maidens, being the daughters of the rabbi of the city, brought the man to their father.

The rabbi greeted him warmly. Then the traveler took the letter from his pocket and handed it to the rabbi, who read it to its end. "Stay with us tonight, and tomorrow I will send you back to your city," he said. "One of us will take you to your king."

"But we have no time to waste, respected Rabbi, for only one day remains of the time period set by the king."

"Do not fear," answered the rabbi. "Before any harm touches a Jew, one of our people will stand before the king." And that very day the rabbi sent heralds to announce: "A great catastrophe has befallen the Jews of a far-off city. Let anyone who wishes to rush to their aid appear before me!" And soon there came before the rabbi one of the Children of Moshe, a one-handed man, blind in one eye, who said, "Send me and I will go." The rabbi received him with joy. He explained the man's duties, gave him his blessing, and, in the morning, sent him off.

Then the man lifted the Jew in his one arm and said, "Shut your eyes tightly."

The Jew did so.

"Open your eyes."

The Jew's eyes opened.

"Tell me now, is this the city of your birth?"

"It is just as you say," answered the Jew in amazement, but to himself he thought, "How could I have gotten back so quickly?"

The emissary of the land of giants set the Jew on his feet. "Tell the king that I am here and am ready to come to the palace." The Jew at once ran off to the rabbi's house, and the rabbi, in turn, rushed to the king, proclaiming, "The man from the Children of Moshe has arrived outside the city gate." To this the king replied, "Then bid him come before me."

Upon being summoned, the emissary of the Children of Moshe entered the city. But, finding the way too narrow, he toppled the buildings obstructing his path. So then a great commotion arose in the city, and the people rushed to the king's palace, crying, "What is happening to us, our King? Are you bent on destroying the city?"

The king, overcome by fright, sent for the rabbi. "Restrain the man from walking any further," he begged. "Let him stand in place and I will come to him." The king called for his chariot, climbed into it—with the rabbi beside him—and soon came near to the emissary from the Children of Moshe. Upon seeing the giant and the aftermath of his deeds, the king felt his own heart lose its fear, and fill instead with honor and esteem. "Return in peace to your birthplace, for I now believe the words of your Torah," he said to the newcomer. "With my own eyes I have seen how one can pursue a thousand, and two cause ten thousand to flee."

May God protect all the cities of Israel!

נר   או אנפאס אן אפסן כרי כרד
דל יוסף בובירין אתהרלן   תיזן אי כן באד ברדאסת
קה סרנו אז הלה סבזש ביראם   בראבסת
לופיש הלהאש קן ענבר   ור אניכת כיסנו מוגענבר   תר

כשידה כישרא אן סבוה   תארי   פנדארי כה בוד אז מושך   ואר
ווריז מוטפה זיורכרי   כרד   אשרא כה מו הד עתאברי   כרד

PURIM

These days should be remembered and kept throughout every generation, every family, every province, and every city; and that these days of Purim should not fall from among the Jews, nor the memorial of them perish from their seed.

—ESTHER 9:28

Everyone loves Purim! This is the day children—and grown-ups too—have been awaiting all year long.

This minor festival falls on the fourteenth day of Adar (usually in the month of March). In Jerusalem it is celebrated on the fifteenth because a rabbinical ruling says that in walled cities a festival is to be observed one day later than elsewhere. In a year when a second month of Adar is added to the calendar, Purim falls in the second Adar.

Adar has always been considered a lucky month because it falls under the zodiac sign Pisces, the fish, a symbol of procreation. It is also a fortunate month because it encompasses Purim, which celebrates the story of the deliverance of the Jews of Persia from the threat of physical destruction. As told in the Book of Esther, the story takes place in an opulent palace laden with gold and silver. The king, Ahasuerus, dismisses his wife and seeks a new one. (Ahasuerus is the Hebrew name for the ruler traditionally thought to be Xerxes I, king of Persia in the fifth century B.C.E.) Esther, a beautiful young girl, is chosen as the new queen; unbeknownst to the king, however, his new wife is a Jewess. The plot thickens when Haman, the king's wicked advisor, schemes to have the Jewish community destroyed. He even draws lots to determine the date of their death (*Purim* in Hebrew means "lots"). But the Jew Mordecai, who is Queen Esther's cousin, tells Esther of this plot. And although revealing her Israelite background could bring about her death, Esther bravely intervenes and makes the king aware of the plight of her people. The Jews are saved and Haman, their enemy, is hanged.

No one knows for sure the source of the Purim story, and scholars offer different theories about it. One holds that Purim is a version of the Babylonian new year festival, when the gods determined the fate of humans by lots, called *puru*. Another theory is that the holiday is related to a Persian feast held in March; except for the similarity of dates, however, there is no connection between the two holidays. A third hypothesis is that the festival arose in the Greek, not the Persian, period of Jewish history and that it is an adaptation of a Greek wine festival.

The atmosphere of this spring partying, following the gloomy winter months, is similar to the frenzied celebrating of Carnival or Mardi Gras

Megillat Esther,
Judeo-Persian
Manuscript,
18th century.
Collection of Isaac
Einhorn,
Tel Aviv/Erich
Lessing/Art
Resource, NY.

The Festival of Deliverance

in Christian countries. The biblical story of Purim does not mention the name of God, but it is understood that there was divine intervention through the brave acts of Esther.

The story has been proven historically inaccurate. For instance, no king named Xerxes ever had a wife named Esther, and there are other inaccuracies as well. In fact, some scholars maintain that the story is no more than historical fiction, created to give validity to the celebration. Nevertheless, inaccurate or not, fictional or not, the story endures and serves as a catharsis for feelings of anger against evil and injustice. Today, the Purim festival is also a time for Jews to ask themselves, "How can we rid ourselves of chauvinism? Of prejudice against other religions?"

The Purim celebration combines religious rulings and an enormous embroidery of folk customs. Indeed, this day has an air of humor, absurdity, parody, and satire not found or permitted on any other day of the year. Another difference is that on Purim candles are not lit, nor is Kaddish recited after a death or on the anniversary of a death. And to insure that the Sabbath is not desecrated by the absurdity and frenzy of the day, Jewish sages calculated the calendar so that Purim never falls on the Sabbath.

All over the world, and for much of Jewish history, men and boys have been required to study most of the year. But on Purim they are released from learning. Instead, they may perform plays (called Purim *spiels* in Germany) about the Purim story or other subjects; in Europe, this custom eventually led to the development of the Yiddish theater. They may also create a Purim Torah, one in which they poke fun at their rabbis. On Purim, humorous songs, often mocking Haman, are sung. And this is the only day when Jews are commanded to imbibe alcohol—until they can no longer tell the difference between "the curse of Haman" and "the blessing of Mordecai."

The primary religious law (*halachah*) for this day is to go to the synagogue—men and women both—on the eve and morning of Purim and there to read aloud the biblical story (also called the Scroll or the Megillah) of Esther; because it's more convenient for most people to attend in the evening, the Megillah is usually read then. In the

Purim, from Sefer Minhagim, Amsterdam, 1707. Courtesy of The Library of The Jewish Theological Seminary of America.

The Purim parade in Israel is called adloyada, *Aramaic for "until he doesn't know." The expression "until he doesn't know" is traditionally taken to mean that a man should drink "until he doesn't know the difference between Haman's curse and Mordecai's blessing." In Hebrew the* gematria *of the first,* arur Haman, *equals the* gematria *of the second,* baruch Mordecai.

story, Haman's name appears fifty-four times, and at each mention, the audience denounces him by drowning out his name—either by turning a noise-maker (*ra'ashan* in Hebrew; *grogger* in Yiddish) or by clapping, shouting, or stamping. The latter may be a remnant of an older custom in which Haman's name was written on the bottom of one's shoes and literally stamped out. A few hundred years ago, the figure of Haman was burned in effigy; sometimes a wax house, with Haman and his family inside it, was ignited at the beginning of the Megillah reading. In Europe, as far back as the fifth century, Jews were accused of burning the Christian cross and the figure, not of Haman, but of Jesus. Still, the custom survived for a few hundred years after that, until it declined. It still continues in some Sephardi Jewish communities.

The Scroll of Esther is read with accompanying blessings, an exception to the usual practice for reading biblical scrolls. The text instructs Jews to bring *mishloach manot* (gifts of food) to friends and family. These usually take the form of tightly filled bags—or platters heaped high—with fruit, sweets, and baked goods. The obligation of having a Purim feast (*se'udah*) is often fulfilled by eating these fruits and sweets. A few hundred years ago, Jews baked Purim cakes in the shapes of the Purim story's characters. Today, Jews bake and devour hamantaschen, three-cornered cakes, whose name in German means "Haman's pockets"; they are shaped like Haman's hat or ears. Some Jews eat kreplach, a meat-filled dough in the same three-cornered shape. Others eat assorted beans as a symbol of Esther's efforts to keep kosher (*kashrut*) at the palace.

A uniquely Jewish aspect of the Purim festival is the commandment to send gifts to the poor. The observance of this obligation (mitzvah) requires even the poorest person to give.

Many people fill hamantaschen, the three-cornered Purim cakes, with poppy seeds because the German and Yiddish word for poppy seeds is mohn, *which sounds like the second syllable of Haman.*

The name Esther probably comes from Istar, a Babylonian goddess. But many people say that the name Esther comes from the Hebrew verb l'hastir להסתיר, *which has the same three-letter root* סתר *as Esther and means "to disguise or hide," as Esther certainly did by not telling her husband that she was a Jewess and as God did by not appearing overtly in the story. The wearing of costumes, disguises, and masks has become part of the Purim celebration.*

THE PURIM GIFT

by Isaac Bashevis Singer

Our home was always half unfurnished. Father's study was empty except for books. In the bedroom there were two bedspreads, and that was all. Mother kept no foods stocked in the pantry. She bought exactly what she needed for one day and no more, often because there was no money to pay for more. In our neighbors' homes I had seen carpets, pictures on the walls, copper bowls, lamps, and figurines. But in our house, a rabbi's house, such luxuries were frowned upon. Pictures and statuary were out of the question; my parents regarded them as idolatrous. I remember that in the *heder* I had once bartered my *Pentateuch* for another boy's, because the frontispiece of his was decorated with pictures of Moses holding the Tablets and Aaron wearing the priestly robe and breastplate—as well as two angels. Mother saw it and frowned. She showed it to my father. Father declared that it was forbidden to have such pictures in a sacred book. He cited the Commandment: "Thou shalt not make unto thee any graven image, or any likeness …." Into this stronghold of Jewish puritanism, where the body was looked upon as a mere appendage to the soul, the feast of Purim introduced a taste of luxury.

All the neighbors sent Purim gifts. From early afternoon the messengers kept coming. They brought wine, mead, oranges, cakes, and cookies. One generous man sent a tin of sardines; another, smoked salmon; a third, sweet-and-sour fish. They brought apples carefully wrapped in tissue paper, dates, figs—anything you could think of. The table was heaped with delicacies. Then came the masked mummers, with helmets on their heads and card-

board shields and swords, all covered with gold or silver paper. For me it was a glorious day. But my parents were not pleased with this extravagance. Once a wealthy man sent us some English ale. Father looked at the bottle, which bore a colorful label, and sighed. The label showed a red-faced man with a blond mustache, wearing a hat with a feather. His intoxicated eyes were full of a pagan joy. Father said, in an undertone, "How much thought and energy they expend on these worldly vanities."

Later in the day Father would treat the Hasidim with the wine. We did not eat the Warsaw cakes, for we were never certain just how conscientious Warsaw Jews were about the dietary regulations. One could not know whether the pastries had been baked with chicken fat and must therefore not be eaten together with any milk foods.

The mummers, too, were disposed of quickly, for the wearing of masks and the singing of songs smacked of the theater, and the theater was *tref*—unclean. In our home, the "world" itself was *tref*. Many years were to pass before I began to understand how much sense there was in this attitude.

But Krochmalna Street did not wish to take note of such thoughts. For Krochmalna Street, Purim was a grand carnival. The street was filled with maskers and bearers of gifts. It smelled of cinnamon, saffron and chocolate, of freshly-baked cakes and all sorts of sweets and spices whose names I did not know. The sweetshops sold cookies in the shapes of King Ahasuerus, Haman the Wicked, the chamberlain Harbona, Queen Vashti, and Vaizatha, the tenth son of Haman. It was good to bite off Haman's leg, or to swallow the head of Queen Esther. And the noisemakers kept up a merry clamor, in defiance of all the Hamans of all the ages.

Among betrothed couples, and boys and girls who were "going with each other," the sending of Purim gifts was obligatory. This was part of the customary exchange of engagement presents. Because of one such Purim gift, an argument arose that almost led to a *Din Torah*, or rabbinical trial, in our house.

A young man sent his betrothed a silver box, but when she opened it—in the presence of her sister and her girl friends, who were impatiently awaiting the arrival of the gift—she found it contained a dead mouse! She uttered an unearthly shriek and fainted. The other girls screeched and screamed. After the bride-to-be had been revived with compresses of cold water and vinegar, and her friends had collected their wits, they began to plot revenge. The bride-to-be knew the reason for her boyfriend's outrageous deed. Several days before, they had quarreled. After much talk and discussion, the young women decided to repay the malicious youth in kind. Instead of a dead mouse, however, they sent him a fancy cake—filled with refuse. The baker was party to the conspiracy. The girls of Krochmalna Street looked upon this conflict as a war between the sexes, and Krochmalna Street had something to laugh about that Purim. The strange part of it was

Noisemaker (grogger), Russia, 19th century. The Jewish Museum, New York/Art Resource, NY.

that the young man, although he had committed a revolting act, had not expected an equally odious retaliation, and was no less stunned than his fiancée had been. People quickly added imaginary incidents. The girls of Krochmalna Street always believed in laughing. One often heard bursts of uncontrolled laughter that might have come from an insane asylum. This time they chortled and chuckled from one end of the street to the other. The young man, too, had been surrounded by friends at the festive Purim meal. He, too, had been aided and abetted in his prank.

Yes, that Purim was a merry one. But the next morning everyone had sobered up and the warring clans came to us for a *Din Torah*. The room was jammed full with people. The bride-to-be had brought her family and her girl friends, and the groom was accompanied by his relatives and cronies. All of them were shouting as they climbed up the stairs, and they kept on shouting for half an hour or more, and my father had yet to learn who was the accuser, who the defendant and what the tumult was about. But while they were yelling, screaming, hurling insults and curses, Father quietly pored over one of his books. He knew that sooner or later they would grow calm. Jews, after all, are not bandits. In the meanwhile, before more time had been wasted, he wanted to know what Rabbi Samuel Eliezer Edels

Purim Celebration, Israel, 19th century.
Collection of Isaac Einhorn, Tel Aviv/Erich Lessing/Art Resource, NY.

meant by the comment in his book, *The Maharsha* : "And one might also say . . . ."

I was present in the room and soon knew all about the affair. I listened attentively to every insult, every curse. There was quarreling and bickering, but every once in a while someone ventured a mild word or the suggestion that it was senseless to break off a match for such foolishness. Others, however, raked up the sins of the past. One minute their words were wild and coarse, but the next minute they had changed their tune and were full of friendship and courtesy. From early childhood on, I have noted that for most people there is only one small step between vulgarity and "refinement," between blows and kisses, between spitting at one's neighbor's face and showering him with kindness.

After they had finished shouting, and everyone had grown hoarse, someone at last related the entire story to my father. Father was shocked.

"Shame! How can anyone do such things? It is a violation of the law: 'Ye shall not make your souls abominable . . . .'"

Father immediately cited a number of Biblical verses and laws. First, it was impious; second, it was loathsome; third, such acts lead to anger, gossip, slander, discord, and what not. It was also dangerous, for the victim, overcome by nausea, might have become seriously ill. And the defilement of edibles, the food which God had created to still man's hunger and over which benedictions were to be recited, was in itself a sacrilege. Father recalled the sage who used to say that he merited long life if only because he had never left bread crumbs lying on the ground. He reminded them that, in order for a cake to be baked, someone had to till the soil and sow the grain, and then rain and dew had to fall from heaven. It was no small thing that out of a rotting seed in the earth a stalk of wheat burst forth. All the wise men of the world together could not create such a stalk. And here, instead of thanking and praising the Almighty for His bounty, men had taken this gift and used it to provoke their neighbors—had defiled what He had created.

Where formerly there had been an uproar, silence now reigned. The women wiped their eyes with their aprons. The men bowed their heads. The girls bashfully lowered their eyelids. After Father's words there was no more talk of a *Din Torah*. A sense of shame and solemnity seemed to have overcome everyone. Out of my father's mouth spoke the Torah, and all understood that every word was just. I was often to witness how my father, with his simple words, routed pettiness, vain ambition, foolish resentment, and conceit.

After Father's admonition the bride- and groom-to-be made peace. The mothers, who just a few minutes before had hurled insults at each other, now embraced. Talk of setting a date for the wedding was heard. My father received no fee, for there had been no actual *Din Torah*. His words of mild reproach had damaged his own livelihood. But no matter, for the weeks between Purim and Passover were a time of relative prosperity for us. Together with the Purim delicacies, the neighbors

had sent a half ruble or a ruble each. And soon the pre-Passover sale of leavened bread would begin.

When the study had emptied, Father called me over and cautioned me to take heed of what may happen to those who do not study the Torah but concern themselves only with the vanities of this world.

The next Sabbath, after the *cholent*, the Sabbath stew, I went out on the balcony. The air was mild. The snow had long since melted. The pavements were dry. In the gutter flowed little streamlets whose ripples reflected the blue of the sky and the gold of the sun. The young couples of Krochmalna Street were starting out on their Sabbath walks. Suddenly the two who had sent each other the ugly gifts passed by. They walked arm in arm, chatting animatedly, smiling. A boy and his girl had quarreled—what of it?

I stood on the balcony in my satin gaberdine and my velvet hat, and gazed about me. How vast was this world, and how rich in all kinds of people and strange happenings! And how high was the sky above the rooftops! And how deep the earth beneath the flagstones! And why did men and women love each other? And where was God, who was constantly spoken of in our house? I was amazed, delighted, entranced. I felt that I must solve this riddle, I alone, with my own understanding.

On Purim

by Rabbi Rami Shapiro

On Purim we don masks and hide
as Esther masked her true identity.
But we put them on only to better take them off.
So accustomed are we to wearing of masks
that we forget the Face that supports them.
But mask wearing is our norm, not our problem;
it is mask removing that is the true challenge of Purim.

To remove our masks, to face one another
     and ourselves as we are:
knots in the singular rope of universe—
this is the work of Purim.

May this Purim find us with the courage
to remove the mask
and perceive the Face.
May this Purim find us ready to look
beyond diversity
to the mirrored unity reflected in each and every soul.

Purim Mask, Ita Aber, 1977-78. Gift of the artist. The Jewish Museum, New York/Art Resource, NY.

PASSOVER

And if the Holy One, praised be He, had not taken our ancestors out of Egypt, then we,
and our children, and our children's children would still be enslaved to Pharaoh in
Egypt. Now even if all of us were scholars, all of us sages, all of us elders, all of us
learned in Torah, it still would be our duty to tell the story of the Exodus from Egypt.

—THE PASSOVER HAGGADAH

Passover (or *Pesach* in Hebrew) is the oldest and most widely celebrated of all Jewish festivals; it is observed for seven days in Israel and by Reform and Reconstructionist Jews everywhere, and for eight days by others in the Diaspora. In ancient times, nomadic (Jewish) shepherds in the wilderness celebrated a spring festival at the time of the full moon by hastily eating a sacrificial goat or sheep in the middle of the night. A completely distinct and separate festival, observed by the entire community in a holy place, was held on the occasion of the spring grain harvest and was called the Festival of Unleavened Bread. Somewhere along the way, the festivals joined together and assumed a historical focus—the deliverance from hundreds of years of slavery in Egypt. The story of this deliverance is found in the Book of Exodus in the Torah. The event was so important that according to the Torah, Pesach (and not Rosh Hashanah) begins the new calendar year. That is why the name of the Hebrew month of Nisan, in which Pesach falls, was taken from its Babylonian counterpart, Nisanu, which means "to start."

The tale of the Israelites' liberation is a story in praise of God, who freed them from slavery in Egypt three thousand years ago. To deliver the people, God sent ten plagues to frighten the Egyptians; the most terrible was the tenth plague, which killed the first-born in every home. To keep the Hebrew babies from being killed, God commanded each Israelite family to paint the doorpost of its house with the blood of a slain lamb; this would be a sign for God to "pass over" that house. (The Hebrew word *pasach* means "to skip over.") Then Moses led the Israelites through the Red Sea to freedom.

All these events—and more—are recalled in a Passover book, the Haggadah, read during a special meal called the seder, the highlight of the festival.

The Seder,
Meichel Pressman,
1950. The Jewish
Museum, New York/
Art Resource, NY.
Gift of Dr. Henry
Pressman.

Jews of the Caucasus Mountains traditionally embroidered a seder plate onto the Passover
tablecloth so that the table was instantly ready for the seder. The custom may have
arisen because it was often difficult to get fresh foods for the seder plate.

The Festival of Freedom

Through the centuries, there have been more than three thousand versions of this book—including editions for children, for women, and for the blind—many beautifully illustrated in a variety of ways. Jews are instructed to read and tell the story from the Haggadah every year, and each person is encouraged to feel as though he or she has been delivered out of Egypt. Only after the destruction of the Second Temple in 70 C.E.—when most Jews were scattered to the Diaspora and when the seder was transferred to the home—did the meal become the foremost symbol of freedom in dispersion. Based on a Hellenistic-Roman dinner, the seder conveyed a distinctly Jewish message: in every generation a destroyer rises up against the Jews, and in every generation the Jews are liberated. Thus, as Jews sustained the Pesach festival, the Pesach festival sustained Jewish life. To some Jews today, the seder means expanding the limits of individual freedom; to others, it means freeing the oppressed. Every year the seder assumes new meaning; perhaps this is why it continues to survive.

For thousands of years, Jews in every corner of the globe, even in the most difficult circumstances—in concentration camps, for example, or in the armed forces—have strived to attend a Passover seder. But could the Passover seder have survived so long and in so many different places without being changed and reinterpreted? Do Jews everywhere observe exactly the same customs? The answer, of course, is no. The holiday's many rituals and laws have been embellished by the specific circumstances and varying cultures in which Jews have lived—and by the creativity of the Jewish people.

While one Jewish family is having its seder, millions of other Jews around the world are doing the same: singing the same songs (perhaps with a different melody), reciting the same prayers, retelling the same story. On the first night of Passover, every Jew at every seder has the feeling of belonging to *k'lal Yisrael*, the great family of Jews all over the globe.

Jewish families have exactly one month after the festival of Purim to prepare for Passover: cleaning, cooking, shopping, and ridding the house of leavened food. Grains that are allowed to leaven (rise),

Seder Plate, Vienna, 1900. Chinese export porcelain. The Jewish Museum, New York/Art Resource, NY.

Traditionally, Jews share matzah with other Jews who cannot afford to bake or buy it. During the American Civil War, soldiers from the North sent matzah to soldiers in the South.

Many Jews place an extra matzah on the plate and recite a special prayer: "This is the matzah of hope for Jews in the world who are not yet free. Next year may they be free."

called *chametz*, are forbidden on Passover; this taboo on leaven symbolizes the haste with which the Israelites fled Egypt, taking with them bread that had had no time to rise. Every crumb must be removed from the house and symbolically "sold" to a non-Jew. (After Passover, they may be redeemed.) Then, after the "sale," there is a final search. This ritual, "searching for *chametz*," or *b'dikat chametz* in Hebrew, is conducted on the night before the seder, accompanying a blessing praising God, "who has commanded us to remove all *chametz*." While one family member holds a candle or flashlight, another uses a feather to sweep the *chametz* (small bits of which have been hidden around the house) onto a wooden spoon. It is then transferred to a paper bag. The next morning, the last *chametz* is taken outdoors and burned.

The special seder plate, which holds foods symbolic of the festival, must be prepared in advance:

karpas, to represent the green of spring and to remind Jews of the bunched greens the Israelites used to splash lambs' blood on their doorposts; the most common greens served are bunched parsley, celery, lettuce, and scallions. The *karpas* is dipped in salt water, vinegar, or lemon juice—a reminder of the bitter and sour life the Israelites led in Egypt—and then a blessing is recited over it.

charoset (*charoses*, as pronounced by Ashkenazi Jews), to symbolize the mortar the Israelites used to build Pharaoh's buildings. *Charoset* consists of chopped apples, nuts, and wine among Ashkenazi Jews; a similar but stickier, spicier, and fruitier mixture, served among Sephardi Jews, is sometimes rolled into bite-sized balls.

z'roa, to remember the Paschal sacrifice; *z'roa* is usually represented by a shankbone of roasted lamb. According to religious law, vegetarians are permitted to use a beet, because it, like lamb, can "bleed."

beitzah, to symbolize the sacrifices at the Temple and mark the coming of spring and new life. Most families display an egg, dyed brown with tea bags or browned in an oven.

maror, to remind participants of the bitterness of slavery. The *maror* consists of sliced or ground horseradish among Ashkenazi Jews; it can be a bunch of romaine lettuce, as in Yemen; artichokes, as in Gibraltar; or potatoes, to signify the bitterness of the lives of Holocaust victims, who groveled for wild potatoes to survive.

The seder plate may also hold additional horseradish or salt water.

The most symbolic food of Passover is matzah, the square or round wafer-like cracker piled on the table during the seder and eaten in lieu of bread during the entire Passover holiday. This food, too, must be prepared—bought or baked—in advance. Matzah is the symbol of freedom, the food that the Israelites took with them in haste when they were told to leave Egypt quickly. At the seder—the meal of freedom—Jews remember the food they ate as freed people.

Matzah must be made of flour and water and baked within eighteen minutes of mixing; after that time, the dough will leaven. This is not an easy task, and over the years, in different places, many methods of preparation have evolved. Some Jews bake matzah in silence (to speed the process and to prevent evil spirits from entering); others bake while reciting the Hebrew alphabet (for extra holiness); hundreds of years ago some incorporated designs of doves and flowers; in later times a small rake was used to make lines or holes. Some Jews still bake *shmureh* matzah, meaning matzah that is "watched" during the entire process, from the growing of wheat until the baking, so that excess water does not enter and cause leavening.

The seder begins just after sundown on the eve of Passover, the fourteenth night of the month of Nisan. The family's finest dishes, silverware, and tablecloth are used for the occasion. Two small bowls—one filled with salt water symbolizing the tears shed by enslaved Jews in Egypt, the other with scented water symbolizing the miracle of Miriam's well—are placed next to the special seder plate. Polished silver candlesticks and an ornate silver cup for the prophet Elijah stand prominently on the table. Before each person's place setting stands a goblet of wine—filled four times during the course of the evening. Beside each goblet is a Haggadah, its pages often stained and creased after years of use. The word *seder* literally means "order," and, indeed, the seder follows a very specific order as outlined in the Haggadah: lighting candles, reciting blessings over the wine and *karpas*, breaking the matzah and hiding the *afikoman*, retelling the story of liberation from bondage in Egypt, and more. One highlight of the evening takes place near the start of the seder when the youngest child present asks or chants the Four Questions, based on one larger question: "How is this night different from all other nights?"

Order of the Seder

Choose a Haggadah from among the beautiful and large variety available to help with these rituals.

- ❖ Light candles before the seder.
- ❖ Recite the blessing over wine.
- ❖ Recite *Sheh-heh-cheh-ya-nu*.
- ❖ Drink the first cup of wine.
- ❖ Wash hands.
- ❖ Recite the blessing over *karpas* (green vegetables), and eat it.
- ❖ Break and hide the middle matzah, the *afikoman*.
- ❖ Symbolically invite the hungry to the seder.
- ❖ Ask the Four Questions.
- ❖ Tell the story of how God freed the Jews from slavery.
- ❖ Begin the answer to the Four Questions with *Avadim hayinu*—"we were slaves."
- ❖ Tell the tale of the Four Sons.
- ❖ Recite the Ten Plagues.
- ❖ Sing *Dayenu*, in praise of God.
- ❖ Explain the symbols of Passover—*Pesach* (the bone), matzah, and *maror*.
- ❖ Recite the blessing over the wine and drink a second cup.
- ❖ Wash hands a second time.
- ❖ Recite the blessings over the matzah and *maror*, and eat the "Hillel Sandwich," *charoset* and *maror* between small pieces of matzah.
- ❖ Eat the Festive Meal.

❖ Search for the *afikoman*.

❖ Recite grace.

❖ Recite the blessing over the wine and drink the third cup.

❖ Welcome the prophet Elijah.

❖ Recite the Hallel and Great Hallel, psalms and prayers in praise of God.

❖ Recite the blessing over the wine and drink the fourth cup.

❖ Proclaim "Next year in Jerusalem!"

❖ End the seder with song.

During the telling of the Exodus story, while the participants recite in unison the ten plagues that God inflicted upon Egypt—blood, frogs, lice, beasts, blight, boils, hail, locusts, darkness, slaying of the firstborn—many Jews dip one pinky into their goblet and toss the wine onto a small dish. Perhaps this is a reminder that the Egyptians who drowned at the Red Sea were also children of God; we should not drink with too much joy (that is, with a full cup).

Not all plagues are sent by God; some are created by humans. The Passover seder is a good time to explore these questions: "What are some modern plagues in our lives [pollution, littering, prejudice]? And how can we rid ourselves of them?"

Although they are not mentioned in the Haggadah, women in the Passover story should be remembered at the seder because they played an important part in the Exodus. A reading at the seder may include the following passage: "Let us remember all the brave women of the Passover story: Yocheved, who gave birth to Moses; Miriam, who led her people to freedom; Shifra and Puah, the brave midwives who refused to drown the male Hebrew babies; Pharaoh's daughter, who saved baby Moses and raised him; and all the Hebrew mothers who took care of their families. The Talmud tractate Sotah says that because of the labors of Hebrew women all the Children of Israel were set free."

According to legend, a well belonging to Miriam followed the Israelites as they wandered through the desert for forty years and provided them with clear, fresh water during the arduous journey. To remember the well and to honor Miriam, some people set on the seder table a bowl or special cup, filled with water scented by flower petals or spices. Sometimes the cup is blue, as was the water of the well.

What Jews eat at the seder depends on where their families come from: Jews whose families hail from the Mediterranean usually make puddings, appetizers, or soups of green vegetables and eggplant; Jews from Eastern Europe use potatoes in stews and puddings; Italian Jews, who love pasta, have found a way to make it that is kosher for Passover—they form the pasta from flour and water and cook it within eighteen minutes; Jews from North Africa traditionally serve spicy food that echoes North African cuisine.

On the other hand, what Jews eat at the seder also depends on what they like. Cookbooks, the Internet,

Afikoman Bag, China, 19th century. Skirball Cultural Center, Los Angeles. Museum Collection. Photograph by John Reed Forsman.

In many parts of the Jewish world, a piece of the afikoman *would be saved for the entire year—sometimes displayed, sometimes hidden in the house or worn on the body— to bring good luck, abundance, or protection from disasters.*

and friends are wonderful sources of recipes from many parts of the world. Ashkenazi Jews serve matzah balls (*knaidlech* in Yiddish) in soup; depending on the individual's taste, these can be made soft or hard, spicy or bland (Jews from Louisiana add gumbo powder), large or small (Jews from some parts of France eat matzah balls as small as buttons). Sephardi Jews serve *mina*, a kind of layered pie made with matzah and meat, or *bimuelos* (matzah cupcakes). At the seder in the White House—the President orders a seder to be conducted every year—matzah kugl, or pudding, is served.

The only constant is that Ashkenazi Jews do not eat rice, corn, beans, or lentils because these can be ground into flour for making *chametz*. Sephardi and Oriental Jews do eat rice, corn, and legumes and consider them a sign of plenty. Most Ashkenazi Jews do not eat lamb on Passover because it is a reminder of the sacrifices of lamb at the Temple. Ethiopian Jews and Samaritans, who follow the laws of the Torah and not later rabbinic teachings, do eat lamb, as indicated in the Torah.

Before the meal, the seder leader takes the middle matzah from a stack of three on the plate (representing the three kinds of Jewish people—Cohens, Levites, and Israelites), breaks it in half, places it in a napkin or cloth envelope, and hides it somewhere in the house. This hidden piece, called the *afikoman*, must be found later in the seder, after the meal, in order for the seder to continue. Children delight in the search, which includes looking everywhere—under chairs and behind plants. When they find the *afikoman*, they refuse to return it unless the adults give them a gift

Sassoon Spanish Haggadah, (fol. 11v), c. 1320. Collection Israel Museum, Jerusalem. Photograph © Israel Museum/ David Harris.

(no wonder this is their favorite part). Then everyone present at the seder must eat some of the *afikoman*, the last food consumed at the meal.

When the main part of the seder has ended, there is still one guest who has not yet arrived: Elijah the Prophet, who on this night visits every seder all over the world. Elijah, believed to be the forebear of the Messiah, comes to bring peace for all Israel. In Jewish lore, Elijah, as God's messenger, helps the pious and the needy. He's even been known to give Passover food to the poor. At this point in the seder, the door is opened so that Elijah may enter, and a special song is sung to welcome him. A beautiful goblet, filled with wine, is waiting for him. (Some Dutch Jews also leave him a piece of matzah.) A Chasidic custom is to pass an empty cup around the table for Elijah, and every person pours a bit of wine into it; thus, symbolically, everyone contributes something to help better the world.

Just as the Exodus story praises God, so too does the end of the seder become a boisterous proclamation of God's greatness: in psalms and prayers; in the unanimous declaration, "Next year in Jerusalem!"; and in the singing of songs. Ashkenazi, Sephardi, and Oriental Jews have their own selections in Hebrew, Aramaic, English, or their own vernacular Jewish language—Ladino, Yiddish, Judeo-Arabic, or Judeo-Persian. A favorite throughout many Jewish groups is "Only One Kid," a lively song that declares the Holy One to be more powerful than any enemy of Israel. And so the seder ends on a joyful note!

A Letter to God

Iranian folktale, retold by Barbara Rush

The festival of Pesach has many prescriptions of religious law—matzah must be made or purchased, new clothes must be worn to ensure that no chametz may have touched them. For many Jews all over the world, obtaining the Passover necessities presents a financial problem. How this problem is solved is the subject of many tales.

Shumel, the clothes presser, put down his heavy iron and sighed in despair. A serious problem kept him from concentrating on his work. The holiday of Pesach was coming, and there was not enough money to make a seder for his family.

Life was hard in the small Persian village where he lived with his wife, Chabas, and their ten little ones. For all the sunlit hours of the day Shumel lifted the iron and pressed, piece after piece, the clothes that the Jews of the town brought to him. Who could count the hours after dark when he sat, under a dimly lit lamp, pressing quickly to finish a job? And yet Shumel did not complain.

But now that the days of Pesach were approaching, he was quite disheartened. "Ah," Shumel thought to himself, "how can we have the holiday without a seder? What will Pesach be like without matzot and wine to put on the table?"

Shumel pressed another sleeve of a shirt and again paused to think. "All year long I have not been able to save an extra coin for the holiday. And now, who will help me? There is no one from whom I can borrow the money."

All afternoon Shumel sat thus, pressing and thinking. "Alas," he said aloud, "I will write a letter to God. Yes, I will ask God for the money."

That very evening, after Shumel finished his day's ironing and ate his evening meal, he took out a piece of fresh paper, lit the lamp, and prepared to write. Now, Shumel was a man of little education and was not accustomed to writing letters of such importance. After all, how often was it that one wrote a letter to God? For a long while he sat and thought. Finally, with a trembling hand, he wrote his simple request.

After Shumel reread the letter and was satisfied with its contents, he sealed it and went to bed, hopeful that God would answer his plea. In the morning before he started his ironing, he took the letter to the post office and went off to his day's work.

The clerk in the post office read the address on Shumel's letter and was quite perplexed. "A letter to God?" he thought to himself. "Where shall I send it?"

The letter was shifted from one clerk to another, each of whom was equally puzzled by the strange address. At last the letter reached the desk of Muhammad Ussif, the postmaster, who opened the envelope and read aloud:

> *Dear God,*
> *The holiday of Pesach is coming,*
> *and I do not have enough money to*

*make a seder for my family. You must
know, God, how hard I have worked
pressing clothes this past year, but I
have not been able to save an extra
coin for the holiday. Believe me, God,
I am embarrassed to ask you for
favors, but there is no one else I can
turn to for help. I have ten children.
For their sakes I am begging you to
send ten lirot.*
   Thank you, God.
   [signed] Shumel

Now, Muhammad Ussif was a man not
usually known for his compassion. But, as
he read the letter, the room became silent,
and even he was touched by the plight of the
poor Jew.

"Take pity on this man!" Muhammad said
quickly, as if afraid that he would soon change
his mind. "Each of us must dig into his pocket
and find a coin for this poor family."

Muhammad and each of his clerks
reached into a pocket and pulled out a coin.
Together nine lirot were counted, and sent in
an envelope to the poor Jew.

Can you imagine Shumel's excitement
when he saw the money? Matzot and wine were
bought for the seder. Chabas was radiant
indeed in her new dress.

And Shumel sat happily at the table, beaming
on his family with feelings of thanks and joy.

Another year passed. Shumel worked hard
day after day, from morning to night, lifting
the iron, pressing the clothes. But, again the
holiday of Pesach approached, and again he did
not have enough money with which to buy
wine, matzot, and other holiday needs. What
could the poor man do? Once again he decided
to write a letter to God.

And so Shumel sat down, took out a clean
piece of paper, pen, and ink, and wrote:

   Dear God,
   *Thank you for the money you sent
us last year for Pesach. My wife
Chabas bought a new dress, and we
all had wine and matzot and good
food for the seder.*
   *You must know that I have worked
hard all year long, but now that the
holiday of Pesach is coming again,
I do not have enough money to make a
seder for my family. If you remember,
God, I have ten children. Please send
us ten lirot, and we will be able to
celebrate properly.*

Shumel was about to sign the letter, but then
he paused, thought quickly, and added a few lines:

   Dear God,
   *I am ashamed to tell you that last
year when you sent the money through
the post office, there were thieves there
who kept one lira for themselves. So this
year I would like to ask a favor of you.
Please, dear God, if it's not too much
trouble, send the money directly to me.*

The Rabbi and the Inquisitor

Eastern European folktale, retold by Nathan Ausubel

For centuries, the days before Passover have been fraught with misfortune for Jews throughout the world. As far back as the first century, Christians accused Jews of murdering a child before Passover in order to use the child's blood for making matzah. In later centuries, these false charges spread to Muslim lands as well. In folktales about such accusations, help often comes via God's intervention; sometimes, as in this story, wit saves the day. —editor's note

The city of Seville was seething with excitement. A Christian boy had been found dead, and the Jews were falsely accused by their enemies of having murdered him in order to use his blood ritually in the baking of *matzos* for Passover. So the rabbi was brought before the Grand Inquisitor to stand trial as head of the Jewish community.

The Grand Inquisitor hated the rabbi, but, despite all his efforts to prove that the crime had been committed by the Jews, the rabbi succeeded in disproving the charge. Seeing that he had been bested in argument, the Inquisitor turned his eyes piously to Heaven and said:

"We will leave the judgment of this matter to God. Let there be a drawing of lots. I shall deposit two pieces of paper in a box. On one I shall write the word 'guilty'—the other will have no writing on it. If the Jew draws the first, it will be a sign from Heaven that the Jews are guilty, and we'll have him burned at the stake. If he draws the second, on which there is no writing, it will be divine proof of the Jews' innocence, so we'll let him go."

Now the Grand Inquisitor was a cunning fellow. He was anxious to burn the Jew, and since he knew that no one would ever find out about it, he decided to write the word "guilty" on both pieces of paper. The rabbi suspected he was going to do just this. Therefore, when he put his hand into the box and drew forth a piece of paper, he quickly put it into his mouth and swallowed it.

"What is the meaning of this, Jew?" raged the Inquisitor. "How do you expect us to know which paper you drew now that you've swallowed it?"

"Very simple," replied the rabbi. "You have only to look at the paper in the box."

So they took out the piece of paper still in the box.

"There!" cried the rabbi triumphantly. "This paper says 'guilty'; therefore the one I swallowed must have been blank. Now, you must release me!"

And they had to let him go.

Seder Night in Bergen Belsen: "Tonight We Have Only Matzah"

Hasidic tale, retold by Yaffa Eliach

A few weeks before Passover, about seventy Jews in the section for foreign nationals in Bergen Belsen organized into a group. Most of them were Hasidic Jews who had arrived at the camp from the Bochnia ghetto. The majority of the people from the Bochnia transport were holders of South American passports; a few held British papers from Eretz Yisrael. They organized the group in order to request flour for baking matzot in honor of the approaching Passover holiday. They addressed their written request to the camp commandant, suggesting that instead of their daily ration of bread they be given flour from which they would bake matzot. In this way they would not strain the camp food supplies. Each of the seventy people signed the petition, and the Rabbi of Bluzhov, Rabbi Israel Spira, an old-timer in Bergen Belsen, was selected as the group's spokesman.

Adolf Haas, the camp commandant, read the petition carefully, then looked at the rabbi with open contempt and ridicule. "I will forward the request to Berlin," he said, after a long silence, while nonchalantly toying with his revolver, "and we will act according to their instructions."

Days passed and there was no reply from Berlin. With each passing day, the signers of the petition became more depressed. Some were convinced that they had made a grave mistake by signing the petition, for in doing so, they separated themselves from the rest of the inmates and probably signed their own death sentence, thus

Baking Matzah, from Sefer Minhagim, Amsterdam, 1723. Courtesy of The Library of The Jewish Theological Seminary of America.

making their own "selection." Knowing from their past experience that the Germans set apart the Jewish holidays as days of terror, torture, and death, the seventy petition signers feared that they would probably be the Passover sacrifice, the Paschal lambs of Bergen Belsen.

Passover was only a few days away and the reply from Berlin had not yet arrived. At the height of their despair, when all hope appeared lost and a bitter fate seemed to be inevitable, two tall S.S. men with two huge dogs briskly entered the section for foreign nationals. They summoned the Rabbi of Bluzhov to the camp commandant. In those dark days a summons by an S.S. officer clearly spelled one thing for a Jew: death. The rabbi parted from his friends and began to recite the Vidduy, the prayer one recites before death, as he walked in the direction of the commandant's office.

Camp cap in hand, the rabbi stood before the commandant and listened to what he had to say: "As always, Berlin is generous with the Jews. You can bake your religious bread." The rabbi remained standing, waiting for the horrible decree to follow the commandant's statement, but to the rabbi's great amazement, none did.

Instead, the commandant called in a few inmates from another section in camp who were already waiting at the office entrance, and ordered them to help the rabbi build a small oven for baking matzot in the section for foreign nationals. The rabbi thanked the commandant and rushed back to the barracks in disbelief that they had indeed been granted permission to bake matzot.

The building of the oven began with feverish haste, the Hasidim fearing that the camp commandant would change his mind at any minute and stop them. In the few days before Passover, matzot were baked from the meager rationed flour, matzot that only in name resembled the pre-World War II matzot baked at home. But the people were thrilled with the shapeless black matzot, especially for the children's sake, so they might see and learn that a holiday is observed even in the Valley of Death.

Passover arrived. A Seder was arranged in one of the barracks. Three-tiered wooden bunk beds served as tables and as traditional seats for reclining. Three precious unbroken matzot were placed on the table. An old, dented, broken pot was used as the ceremonial Seder plate. On it there were no roasted shank bone, no egg, no haroset, no traditional greens, only a boiled potato given by a kind old German who worked at the showers.

But there was no shortage of bitter herbs; bitterness was in abundance. The suffering of the Jews was reflected in their eyes.

The Rabbi of Bluzhov sat at the head of the table. He was surrounded by a group of young children and a few adults. The rabbi began to recite the Haggadah from memory.

He uncovered the matzot, lifted the ceremonial plate, and began to tell the story of the Exodus.

This is the bread of affliction that our fathers ate in the land of Egypt. All who are hungered—let them come and eat, all who are needy—let them come and celebrate Passover. Now we are here; next year may we be in the land of Israel! Now we are slaves; next year may we be free men!

The youngest of the children asked the Four Questions, his sweet childish voice chanting the traditional melody: "Why is this night different from all other nights? For on all other nights we eat either bread or matzah, but tonight only matzah."

It was dark in the barracks. The moon's silvery, pale glow was reflected on the pale faces. It was as if the tears that silently streamed down their cheeks were flowing toward the legendary angel with the huge jug of tears, which when filled to its brim would signal the end of human suffering.

As is customary, the rabbi began to explain the meaning of Passover in response to the Four Questions. But on that Seder night in Bergen Belsen, the ancient questions of the Haggadah assumed a unique meaning.

"Night," said the rabbi, "means exile, darkness, suffering. Morning means light, hope, redemption. Why is this night different from all other nights? Why is this suffering, the Holocaust, different from all the previous sufferings of the Jewish people?" No one attempted to respond to the rabbi's questions. Rabbi Israel Spira continued.

"For on all other nights we eat either bread or matzah, but tonight only matzah. Bread is leavened; it has height. Matzah is unleavened and is totally flat. During all our previous sufferings, during all our previous nights in exile, we Jews had bread and matzah. We had moments of bread, of creativity,

Three Haggadahs (written from memory and drawn by the family of Albert Neher, hiding under Nazi occupation), France, 1941-43. Collection of Andre Neher, Jerusalem/Erich Lessing/Art Resource, NY.

and light, and moments of matzah, of suffering and despair. But tonight, the night of the Holocaust, we experience our greatest suffering. We have reached the depths of the abyss, the nadir of humiliation. Tonight we have only matzah, we have no moments of relief, not a moment of respite for our humiliated spirits . . . . But do not despair, my young friends."

The rabbi continued in a forceful voice filled with faith. "For this is also the beginning of our redemption. We are slaves who served Pharaoh in Egypt. Slaves in Hebrew are *avadim* ; the Hebrew letters of the word *avadim* form an acronym for the Hebrew phrase: David, the son of Jesse, your servant, your Messiah. Thus, even in our state of slavery we find intimations of our eventual freedom through the coming of the Messiah.

"We who are witnessing the darkest night in history, the lowest moment of civilization, will also witness the great light of redemption, for before the great light there will be a long night, as was promised by our Prophets. 'But it shall come to pass, that at evening time there shall be light,' and 'The people that walked in darkness have seen a great light; they that dwelt in the land of the shadow of death, upon them hath the light shined.' It was to us, my dear children, that our prophets have spoken, to us who dwell in the shadow of death, to us who will live to witness the great light of redemption."

The Seder concluded. Somewhere above, the silvery glow of the moon was dimmed by dark clouds. The Rabbi of Bluzhov kissed each child on the forehead and reassured them that the darkest night of mankind would be followed by the brightest of all days.

As the children returned to their barracks, slaves of a modern Pharaoh amidst a desert of mankind, they were sure that the sounds of the Messiah's footsteps were echoing in the sounds of their own steps on the blood-soaked earth of Bergen Belsen.

A Journey to Jerusalem

Ethiopian folktale, retold by the North American
Conference on Ethiopian Jewry

This expedition took place in Ethiopia in 1852, when the
British fought the Ethiopian Emperor Theodorus.

It came to pass in the reign of Emperor Theodorus, when the Jews of Ethiopia were led by the wise Aba Mahari, that much anguish came upon the Jewish community. Missionaries were active in their villages, troubling the spirits of the people. Then a decree went out from the Emperor that the Jews must come to his court to debate the missionaries.

Now, Aba Mahari was a man of sixty years. Some say he himself led the great debate in the Emperor's court. Others say he sent his wisest counselors. But all agree the Jews were the victors, and the missionaries became enraged, threatening force against them. And the people were afraid.

Now, Aba Mahari had a dream that the Jews would go to Jerusalem. He dressed in his long white robes, took his staff in his hand, and went to Emperor Theodorus. The Emperor received him kindly, for Aba Mahari had foretold that he would be king while he was still unborn. He said to Aba Mahari, "You are like my father. If you will change your religion, you shall be head of the Church of all Ethiopia." "But," Aba Mahari said, "I cannot do as you ask. Therefore I ask you to send me to Jerusalem with my people. Let me take them home."

And Emperor Theodorus consented, and issued a decree that no one should hinder the Jews.

And so word went out to the Jewish villages in Gondar, Dembia, Tigrel, Quara, and everywhere in Ethiopia—all those who wanted to remain Jews should follow Aba Mahari. And so thousands of Jews walked in the footsteps of Aba Mahari, toward the shores of the Red Sea.

But the long road was filled with obstacles, rivers and mountains. The rainy season came, and many Jews perished of cold and hunger. In the village of Madvay there is to this day a great memorial to the Jews buried there. And the good people of Madvay sought to comfort the Jews

Moses Leading the Israelites Through the Red Sea, from the Haggadah in the Hamburg Miscellany (Cod. Heb. 37 fol. 29v), Germany, 1427. Staats- und Universitätsbibliothek, Hamburg.

by holding a "tazkar" for the dead. Some of the Jews were indeed comforted and turned back saying, "It is as if we have reached Jerusalem. Why? We have heard all your singing, all your praying, all your beating of drums, and we have rejoiced."

But many did not turn back, and went on until they came to the shores of the Red Sea. Then Aba Mahari took his staff, like Moses, and struck the sea so it would open. But the sea did not open. Then those who remembered the story of Nahshon at the time of the Exodus from Egypt—for Nahshon walked boldly into the waters, and they parted—leaped into the sea and began to swim.

Still the waters did not part, and they returned to the shore saying, "Even if we swim to the other side, how can the women and children cross, and those who can't swim?" So they sought a rich woman who lived nearby, to hire her boats, but the boats were not strong enough.

Then the people lost heart, and turned away from Jerusalem to go home. And the journey south was more arduous than the journey north, for plague broke out and many died. To this day none can tell how long the Jews underwent the vicissitudes, the sufferings, and the deaths of their companions before they reached their homes or settled where they fell.

And Aba Mahari, it is said, spent the rest of his life wandering from place to place, to comfort his people and to defend Judaism in Ethiopia.

And so ended the first great Exodus of the Jews of Ethiopia. Some might say that the vicissitudes, the sufferings, and the deaths were in vain, for the Jews did not cross the Red Sea. But to this day, their descendants tell the story, and remember not only the pain their ancestors suffered, but the kindness they met along the way, and the courage of Aba Mahari who walked before them in his old age and did not leave them undefended.

And today, their descendants who are indeed in the Land of Israel and the City of Jerusalem—who crossed the Red Sea in our time, not on land but in the air, borne on the wings of eagles—they say, "Aba Mahari had a vision, and the vision was true. But what he saw was not for his time but for the future. They did not arrive, they were not privileged to reach their goal. But because of their courage and their virtue—we, their children, have arrived."

ELIYAHU THE PROPHET

by Sholom Aleichem, translated by Aliza Shevrin

It isn't good to be an only child, to be doted on anxiously by your father and mother, "of seven the only one remaining." Here—don't stand, there—don't go. This—don't eat, that—don't drink. Your head—cover it, your throat—wrap it. Your hands—hide them. Your nose—blow it. Ah, it isn't good, it just isn't good to be an only child. And a rich man's son at that. My father is rich. He's a money-changer. He goes around from shop to shop with a sack of coins exchanging silver for small change and small change for silver. That's why his fingers are always black and his nails chipped. He works very hard. When he comes home at night he is exhausted and worn out. "My legs are finished," he moans to my mother. "My legs are finished. There's nothing left of my legs."

Nothing left? It's possible. But then again, his business is thriving. That's what everyone says, and everyone is envious of us because the business is good and very good at that. My mother is pleased. So am I. "The kind of Pesach I will have this year, I wish for all Jewish children, God be praised."

Passover Goblet, Netherlands, 18th century. Judaica Collection of Max Berger, Vienna/Erich Lessing/Art Resource, NY.

That's what my mother says and she thanks God because we are having such a wonderful Pesach. And I do too. But how am I going to make it through the days until that wonderful seder?

I barely make it to Pesach, that beloved Pesach. They have outfitted me like a king, as befits a rich man's son. But what good is it? I am not allowed to play outdoors—I might catch a cold. I am not allowed to run around with the poor children—I am a rich man's son. Such beautiful clothes and no one to show them off to. A pocketful of nuts and no one to play with.

It's no good to be an only child, overprotected, of seven the only one remaining and a rich man's son at that.

My father puts on his best long coat and goes off to *shul* to pray. My mother says to me, "Do you know what? Lie down a little. Take a little nap. Then you'll be able to stay up with us for the whole seder. You will ask your father the Four Questions." Am I crazy? Do you think I could sleep before a seder? "Remember now, at the Pesach seder you are not allowed to fall asleep, because if, God forbid, you do fall asleep, then right away Eliyahu the Prophet will appear with a big sack on his back. Pesach night Eliyahu the Prophet goes around looking for anyone who falls asleep at the seder and takes him away in his sack." Ha-ha! I fall asleep at the seder? I? Even if it lasts all night, until the crack of dawn. What happened last year, Momma? "Last year you fell asleep right after the *Kiddush*." So how come Eliyahu the Prophet didn't come to me with his sack then? "Then you were only a little boy but this year you are a big boy, this year you are old enough to ask your father the Four Questions. This year you have to recite along with your father the *Avadim hayinu*—'Slaves were we.' This year you have to eat fish and soup and knaidlach with us. Quiet—here comes your father from *shul*."

"*Goot yontiff*!"

"*Goot yontiff*!"

Thank God. My father finishes reciting the *Kiddush*. So do I. My father drinks down the first glass of wine. So do I. And a full one at that, down to the last drop. "Look at that, down to the last drop!" my mother exclaims to my father, and then she says to me, "A full glass of wine? You'll fall asleep!" Ha-ha! *I* fall asleep? *I*?

Even if it lasts all night, until the crack of dawn. Just ask Poppa how well I polished off the Four Questions, how well I read the Haggadah, how I swayed back and forth over the *siddur* and sang the *Avadim hayinu*. My mother keeps her eyes glued to me and smiles as she says to me, "You will fall asleep, fall asleep. . . ." Ah, Momma, Momma! It seems to me that if a person had eighteen heads, just hearing those words would make him fall asleep! Just try to stay awake when you have the words, "Fall asleep, fall asleep . . ." sung into *your* ear.

Obviously, I fall asleep.

I fall asleep and dream that my father is already at the portion of the *Haggadah Sh'foach chamt'chah*. My mother is getting up from the table to open the door in order to welcome Eliyahu the Prophet. That would be a fine how-do-you-do if Eliyahu the Prophet were to come in, as my mother described, with a sack on his back and say to me, "Come, young man." And whose fault would it be? Momma's—because of her "Don't fall asleep! Don't fall asleep." And

Passover Kiddush Cup, Johann Hoffler, Nuremburg, Germany, c. 1698. Gift of Miriam and Arnold Frankel. Photograph by Malcolm Varon. The Jewish Museum, New York/Art Resource, NY.

just as I am thinking these thoughts—Aha!—I hear the scraping of the door and my father stands up and calls out loud, "Welcome!" I look toward the door and sure enough—yes, it's him. He's walking toward me, walking toward me—so slowly, you can barely hear him. He's a fine-looking Jew, Eliyahu the Prophet. An old man. An old man with a curly gray beard down to his knees. The face is aged, yellowed, wrinkled but handsome and filled with goodness. And his eyes—ah, his eyes! Gentle, kind, friendly, loving, trusting eyes. Bent over, leaning on a huge staff, with a sack on his back, he silently, oh so silently, without a word, comes straight toward me.

"Well, young man, climb into my sack and come with me!" So says this old man to me and yet with such kindness, with such gentleness, such sweetness.

I ask him, "Where to?" He responds, "You'll know soon enough." I don't want to, but he bids me to come again. I plead with him. "How can I go with you when I am a rich man's son?" He replies, "So if you are a rich man's son, what's so special about that?" I go on, "I am my parents' only child." This does not impress him. "To me you're not an only child." I try again. "But I am watched over, of seven the only one remaining. If they see that I'm gone," I continue, "they will not endure it. They will die—especially my mother." He gazes at me, the old man, with benevolence in his eyes, and says to me as gently and sweetly as before, "If you don't come with me, then sleep soundly but sleep forever, forever." I begin to cry. "Does that

mean I will die? They won't endure it, especially Momma." "If you don't want to die, then come with me. Say goodbye to your parents and come." "But after all, how can I go when I am an only child, of seven the only one remaining?" Now he becomes a little more stern. "For the last time, young man, decide one way or the other: either you say goodbye to your mother and father forever and come with me or stay here, but fall asleep forever. Forever."

Having said these words, he takes a step away from me and is about to go out the door. What should I do now? Go with the old man. God knows where, to be eternally lost? My parents would die. An only child, of seven the only one remaining. Stay here and sleep forever? That means I myself would die. I stretch both hands out pleadingly to him with tears in my eyes. "Eliyahu the Prophet! Good, beloved, generous Eliyahu! Give me one minute to think about it!" He turns his fine, old, yellowed, wrinkled face, with the curly gray beard down to his knees, toward me, looks at me with his fine, good, loving, trusting eyes, and says to me with a smile, "I will give you one minute to think about it, my child, but no more than one minute."

And the old man leans on his huge staff and waits.

Now I ask you—in that one minute, what could I possibly think that would permit me not to go with the old man and yet not sleep forever? Just go ahead. Try to guess!

*W*hen you enter the land that I am giving to you, and you reap its harvest, you shall bring the first sheaf of the harvest to the priest. He shall elevate the sheaf before the Lord for acceptance in your behalf.

—LEVITICUS 23:10, 11

Shavuot, David Sharir, 1981. Courtesy of the artist.

FOUR

Completing the Circle of the Year:
From Late Spring to Summer

Counting the omer is not a festival; rather, it is a time period that includes many festivals. The custom of counting the omer (the omer is, literally, the measure of barley to be counted) has biblical origins. From the second day of Pesach, there are seven weeks of seven days in which the earth unfolds and the grain grows. Farmers in biblical times, hoping that the harvest would succeed and worrying that it might fail, counted the days until the first harvest could be expected to ripen. This period of counting, called *Sephirat Ha Omer* in Hebrew, ended on the fiftieth day, Shavuot. Then the ceremony would take place, as described in the passage from Leviticus (on page 128), in which two loaves of bread were waved as an offering to God, to celebrate the end of the weeks of anxiety.

The rabbis in ancient times saw an additional meaning in this celebration: it was an ascent from the political liberation of Pesach to the spiritual revelation at Shavuot. Therefore, even after the destruction of the Temple, the rabbis decreed that the omer counting should continue.

Omer Scroll, Holland, c. 1680. Gift of Harry G. Friedman. The Jewish Museum, New York/ Art Resource, NY.

This period of the omer counting later acquired meaning as a time of limited mourning: no performing of marriages, cutting of hair, wearing of new clothing, or entering a new house are allowed at this time, except on Lag B'Omer, the thirty-third day of counting. The reasons for mourning are unclear: perhaps Jews were asked to lament the destruction of the Temple or the dead soldiers of the second-century commander against Rome, Simeon bar Kochba. They may also have been asked to lament the many students of Rabbi Akiba, the great second-century sage, who are said to have died of plague during this time.

Folk artists have made many beautiful charts to help with the counting and to give visual form to this period of time. On the six Sabbaths during this seven-week period, chapters of *Ethics of the Fathers* (*Pirkei Avot*) are read. The Talmud tractate Shavuot is studied not only because the name is the same as the festival's but also because it contains forty-nine pages, the same as the number of days of counting.

On the Sabbath after Pesach, when the dates of the new month of Iyar are announced, some Jews make a challah in the shape of a key—a key to the new month of Iyar. Some people sprinkle the challah with sesame seeds as a reminder that during this month manna began to fall for the Children of Israel as they wandered in the desert.

In modern times, the period of the counting of the omer has become a time to reflect on the world food situation: "Just as God sustained us with manna, are we not able to sustain the people of the planet?" Thus, it is a time to support groups that work toward relieving hunger.

The three newest holidays in the Jewish year—Holocaust Remembrance Day, Israel Independence Day, and Jerusalem Day—fall in the period of counting the omer. The Israeli Knesset has declared each of these days a holiday of observance. When creating these new holidays, the people looked to their familiar religious roots—to the Bible, to prayers—and to previous customs, such as the lighting of candles, the eating of certain foods, and the singing of songs, which they then incorporated into the new celebrations.

Among the Jews of Libya, on the second night of Pesach, cubes of salt—called omer salt—are distributed in the synagogue. Each night as the omer is counted, the salt is held. It is believed to have the miraculous powers of protecting people from harm; when thrown into the sea, it keeps ships from colliding.

LAG B'OMER

Beat your plowshares into swords,

And your pruning-hooks into spears;

Let the weak say: "I am strong."

—JOEL 4:10

More Torah,

more life.

—ETHICS OF THE FATHERS, 2:8

The minor festival of Lag B'Omer occurs on the thirty-third day of the counting of the omer; the name means the thirty-third day of counting, because the word *lag* has, according to *gematria*, the numerical value 33 in the Hebrew alphabet. In order to Judaize an ancient heathen forest festival marked by ceremonial bonfires, the Talmudic rabbis, and those of the next few centuries, connected the festival with events in Jewish history, namely the lives of three second-century heroes: Simeon bar Yochai, Simeon bar Kochba, and Rabbi Akiba.

During the second century, while the Romans ruled Palestine, Jews were forbidden to teach and practice Judaism.

On Lag B'Omer, in Meron in northern Israel, bonfires burn brightly, sending their leaping flames high into the air. This is the site of the grave of Simeon bar Yochai, a second-century sage and mystic who is said to have performed many miracles and can still work miracles all year long for those in need. On this day, thousands and thousands of people come by bus, by car, or by anything else that will travel to beseech the

Omer Calendar, Maurice Mayer, Paris, c. 1870. Skirball Cultural Center, Los Angeles. Museum Collection. Photograph by John Reed Forsman.

The menorah of bar Yochai was taken to the island of Djerba off the coast of Tunisia by Jews who landed there after the bar Kochba rebellion in the second century. Because of the menorah's miraculous powers—it has saved Jews and Arabs alike from destruction—the synagogue where it stands is a holy place for both peoples.

A Day for Remembering Courage

sage, "Bring an end to my barrenness" or "Send a cure for my physical infirmity."

According to legend, when the Roman emperor Hadrian threatened bar Yochai with death because of his teaching of Torah, the sage and his son took refuge in a cave. They lived for thirteen years, dining only on the fruit of a carob tree that miraculously appeared, and they quenched their thirst at a stream that appeared in the same manner. While there, the legend says, the two men were visited by Elijah the Prophet, who taught them heavenly secrets. After the emperor's death, bar Yochai resumed his role as teacher, imparting the Torah and various mystical lessons to those gathered around him. All this time, the legend continues, a protective fire burned around his academy, barring unworthy persons from entering. So great were bar Yochai's teachings that they became the foundation for the basic text of Jewish mysticism, the *Zohar* (meaning "splendor").

When bar Yochai died (on Lag B'Omer), a rainbow is said to have appeared in the sky. In Hebrew, the word *keshet* can mean either a rainbow or a hunter's bow; this duality of meaning is one of the reasons that Jews in Eastern Europe took to the woods on Lag B'Omer to practice their skills with bows and arrows.

All over Israel, on the eve of Lag B'Omer, bonfires burn high—in memory of the protective fire of bar Yochai or, more probably, of the ancient bonfires of the forest festival—as people congregate for picnics. During the day, those who cannot travel to Meron visit the graves of other sages.

Lag B'Omer also commemorates Simeon bar Kochba, commander of the rebellion of Palestinian Jews against Rome. On the thirty-third day of the counting of the omer, bar Kochba's soldiers captured Jerusalem, although the rebellion was eventually unsuccessful. Traditionally, on Lag B'Omer, students in Eastern Europe went out to the fields or woods with bows and arrows, bar Kochba's weapons; the popularity of archery on Lag B'Omer reflects an attempt to emulate bar Kochba's physical prowess. Today, many athletic events take place on Lag B'Omer, both in the United States and Israel.

The third hero is the famed Rabbi Akiba, a great sage of the second century. During the weeks between Pesach and Shavuot, thousands of his students died of a fatal epidemic; on Lag B'Omer, it is said, the deaths ceased. To remember the students who died of plague, Jews observe mourning customs during the weeks between Pesach and Shavuot. One of the most stringent is the prohibition of marriages during this time. But on Lag B'Omer, just as the deaths ceased, the mourning customs cease as well; marriages may be performed on this day. Note that Lag B'Omer falls between Independence Day and Jerusalem Day.

RABBI SHMUEL THE CANDLE LIGHTER

Israeli folktale, retold by Barbara Rush

Every week, before Shabbat, it was the custom of Rabbi Shmuel to go from Safed to Meron and light candles at the grave of Rabbi Shimon bar Yochai. In those days, the road from Safed to Meron was beset with dangers: bandits, beasts of prey, and furious rainstorms that fell during winter. But no power in the world could prevent Rabbi Shmuel from lighting candles at the grave of the saintly man. In the course of twenty years he had never missed a single visit before Shabbat.

About fifty years ago the winter was harsh. Heavy snow fell for a week; frozen by intense cold, it was too slippery to walk on. But Rabbi Shmuel set out as usual. There was not a path, not a house, not a tree: a sparkling white carpet covered all. Rabbi Shmuel continued on his way, heavily dragging his feet.

Rabbi Shmuel went to the courtyard of Rabbi bar Yochai, but much snow had piled up, making the gate impossible to open. Sweeping the snow with his hands, he used his frozen fingers to wipe away the sweat that had dropped into his eyes, when, suddenly, there appeared another Jew who began to remove the snow. And miracle of miracles: every spot of snow that was touched by the fingers of this stranger melted at once, as if a bonfire had been lit there. After a few minutes the snow was gone; the way to the gate and the grave was clear.

"I am glad you came," said the stranger. "I was afraid that no one would come out in this snow to light a Shabbat candle at the grave of Shimon bar Yochai, so I came myself."

Rabbi Shmuel entered bar Yochai's chamber, lit the candles, and then went out to look for the stranger. But the man had disappeared. Rabbi Shmuel searched for him to no avail—and then headed out to follow his own footsteps back to his house in Safed.

But the snow continued to fall. The way became even more difficult; the hour grew late; the cold sun sank. Rabbi Shmuel feared that he might not manage to reach Safed before the coming of Shabbat. His family would worry, and the joy of their Shabbat would be disturbed.

Then, suddenly, he heard the growling of beasts of prey. The blood froze in his veins: "Father in heaven, please help me. Save me, by virtue of the saintly Rabbi Shimon bar Yochai."

And just as he finished his prayer, there appeared, once again, the same Jewish stranger whom he had met at the courtyard of bar Yochai. The Jew motioned for Rabbi Shmuel to follow. And once again a miracle occurred: wherever the man set foot, the snow quickly melted.

After a few minutes, Rabbi Shmuel's feet stood in the courtyard of his own home. He opened the door and entered the warm, pleasant house. He wanted to invite the stranger inside, but, once again, the man had vanished. It was as if he had never existed.

Silver Tetradrachma from the bar Kochba Revolt. Collection Israel Museum, Jerusalem.

HOLOCAUST REMEMBRANCE DAY

"You shall blot out the memory of Amalek from under heaven. Do not forget!"

—DEUTERONOMY 25:19

The aura of this secular day is holy and solemn, as Jews collectively remember, mourn, and honor the millions who were killed in the Holocaust. In the Diaspora, it is observed on April 19, the anniversary of the uprising in the Warsaw ghetto. The Israeli Knesset designated the twenty-seventh of the month of Nisan for celebration.

Holocaust Remembrance Day (*Yom Ha Sho'ah* in Hebrew) has no biblical or rabbinical roots and therefore no religious sanction; nor is its observance clearly defined. Yet all over the world, in Israel and in the Diaspora, people feel compelled to hold services, to light memorial candles, and to recite Kaddish for the deceased. Often, survivors (and their offspring) from the same ghetto, camp, or city gather to say Kaddish in unison. Holocaust Remembrance Day is a time to reflect on questions of good and evil and on God's role in the world.

In Israel, at 10:00 A.M. a siren sounds, and every person, everywhere in the country—in a store or car, at home or at work—stops and stands at attention to honor the dead and to share in a moment of silent solidarity.

At some point people decided that yellow tulips should be displayed on this day. Perhaps yellow signifies the Star of David that Jews were forced to wear, and tulips symbolize spring rebirth; or tulips may suggest Holland, where they are grown and where citizens actively tried to save Jews during World War II.

Many people eat a symbolic meal of rotten bread, potato peels, and diluted soup, the food of Jewish prisoners during the Holocaust. Among songs associated with the day are *Ani Ma'amin* ("I Believe"), traditionally sung at the Yizkor service on the High Holy Days, and "Hymn of the Partisans," a Yiddish song of hope and defiance that spread throughout the concentration camps and ghettos.

In the United States, Holocaust Remembrance Day is a time for mass meetings in synagogues and secular settings, characterized by the lighting of candles, speeches, songs, and testimonies of Holocaust victims. Participants read from the works of Elie Wiesel, Victor Frankl, Anne Frank, or from other volumes of Holocaust literature. Holocaust museums offer films, theatrical performances, and observances. In the United States, the president attends a Holocaust Remembrance ceremony in Washington, D.C.

Self-portrait with Jewish Identity Card, Felix Nussbaum, 1943. Kulturgeschichtliches Museum Osnabruck. © Auguste Moses-Nussbaum and Shulamit Jaari.

In Jewish life, lighting a candle commemorates the passing away of a soul. On Holocaust Remembrance Day, people light six candles, one for each million killed. Sometimes there is a seventh candle, to honor non-Jewish victims or Gentiles who saved Jewish lives; this seventh candle, because of the sacred nature of the number seven, is one way of giving the day's observances a religious significance.

A New Holiday

A Star-Crossed Childhood

by Rosy Abelson

The sky was mysteriously lit that afternoon. Heavy clouds hung over our heads and a fine drizzle was wetting our faces, yet somewhere on the right the sunrays were tearing the sky, letting luminous trails of light dance over the golden church domes of St. Sofia. What a day! Bulgarian peasants say that mountain bears marry in weather like that. I tried to imagine a bear marriage for just a very short while, though I knew it was a lot of nonsense and this was no time to waste on frivolous fantasy strolls. Today was important, very important. My whole family, that is, mother, father, Ruth (my sister), and I were on our way to an appointment in the church, Santa Sofia, to be converted to Christianity. We had to convert because we were Jewish; not only us, our little family, but all the others: grandpa, grandma, all my uncles, aunts and cousins, everybody was a Jewish Bulgarian, rather than a Bulgarian Bulgarian! We, though, were the only ones who were going to try conversion, and I guess my father had made his decision because things had been getting unpleasant lately. That is, many Bulgarian Bulgarians stopped liking Jewish Bulgarians and were causing a lot of trouble. It was clear to me that if we got converted, life would revert to what it had been before that abominable war had started. It was all very simple. We would become Orthodox Christians, go to church on Sunday, and be like everybody else. Thoughts were crowding my head, pushing and shoving, new exhilarating possibilities, yet I was constrained to keep my joy to myself because my mother, my lovely sweet mother, did not understand the whole affair and had been walking with swollen and red eyes for the last two days. The previous night, I heard her tell father: "What am I going to tell them, this will kill

them, you know my father and what all that means to him." My father kept repeating, "We have no choice, Rachel, we have to think of the children." The children of course were my sister, Ruth, a perfect pest, age five, and myself, mature and thoughtful, age ten. We spent the whole morning preparing for the church appointment and it is a real miracle that we got out of the house at all. Ruth had a fit because she did not want to give up her golden Star of David and because she did not like her new Bulgarian name, "Bojidarka." But things quieted down and we all dressed up in our best clothes. We all looked lovely. Especially me. I was wearing my plaid, pleated dress, my blue coat with the velvet collar, hand-knitted white socks and my new patent leather shoes. It was very hard to keep clean in such weather. My eyes were fixed on the shiny tips on my shoes. I stepped with care, avoiding mud and puddles, determined to keep the best possible appearance for the great occasion.

When we reached the church we were slightly taken aback. There was a long line of people already waiting in front of the closed metal doors. In answer to our inquiries, we were told that we had to wait on line like everybody else and that conversions seemed to go very slowly. I was not particularly bothered. We were used to standing on line. I was the one that bought bread every day, which took at least an hour or two. Thus I discovered that there were lots of things one could do while standing on lines. One could find a new friend to chat with, read, or even simply daydream. This day I chose to daydream. There were so many things to remember to hope about. I embarked on my favorite fantasy:

I am a Christian and I can make the sign of the

cross; then every morning at the end of the fifteen minute long prayer, when Sister Josepha, the grammar teacher from French Catholic School, says "In the name of the Father, the Son, and the Holy Ghost, Amen," I join the rest of the class and close my eyes and repeat those mysterious, now forbidden words "Au nom du Père et du Fils et du Saint Esprit, ainsi Soit-il . . ." and touch my forehead, repeating in enchantment the magical configuration of the cross . . . . Oh how wonderful it could be. And that is not all. My friend, Lilette, made the sign of the cross before every exam and she claimed that it helped a lot. She thought that all prayers were more effective that way and I always felt deprived of a kind of booster to my prayers. Tatiana, who shared a bench with me, kept her fingers crossed whenever she told white lies, because as long as you harm nobody and you cross yourself in secret it is all right. Ah, all these new

and wonderful things that were about to happen! But with all the rejoicing going on inside of me I was carefully avoiding my parents' faces lest they notice my exuberance. Mama and Tatko (father) looked very grim and as for Ruthy, she kept pestering everybody with her usual round of demands: she wants water, she is sleepy, she is hot, no she is cold, she is tired, etc., just her ordinary, usual self. To keep her spirits up I called her by her new Bulgarian name: "Bojidarka, Bojidarka," but this joke ended in yells and screams, proving again what a pest she was. Time slowly passed and it became cold and damp. The sun had disappeared long ago and the crowd was silent and depressed. The huge metal

doors of the church remained firmly closed only to open for mysterious people, who would enter hurriedly or leave. Frankly, it did not seem as if the priests were particularly efficient inside the church. But all we could do was to patiently persevere, perseverance being a most valued virtue in those days. Then suddenly a little man dressed in a dark overcoat and a soft top hat hurriedly approached a group of people waiting in line. He appeared to be the bearer of important news and whatever he was saying caused a lot of excitement and commotion. My father ran to him and asked in anguish, "What is going on?" "They are making black lists," the little man answered, "and the converted go first. The churches are sending the list of names straight to the Commissariat for Jewish Affairs." There was hardly any need to explain more. Even I understood that it would be better not to be seen near a church. I had rarely seen my father act with greater speed. He turned to mama and said, "Let's go Rachel, where the rest go, we go!" My mother agreed silently. Tatko picked Ruthy up in his arms, embracing her little body tight against his chest and holding her head against his shoulder; he began running like a madman, turning occasionally to see if mother and I were following. I was watching my sister's pigtails flowing in the air while mother kept pulling my arm saying, "Hurry now, hurry."

Out of breath, we found ourselves in the small room that was home in those days. It was only then that I realized what had happened. It was all over. The possibility of having a passport for sameness in the world was lost forever. I hung my coat in the hall, then sat on my bed and looked at my muddy shoes and the big grey spots on my white socks. Obviously, they were ruined completely. I began crying softly, trying to restrain the pain pressing against my chest. Ruthy looked at me with great worry, then put her tiny paw on my face, smearing the tears on my cheek, which pained me even more. Suddenly I felt an overwhelming tenderness for her, for myself, for mama and Tatko and all the others. Mama asked, "What is all that moping around?" I said I cried because I loved them and because my white hand-knitted socks were ruined forever; the spots would never come off. Mama said, "Ha, ha, such silly reasons for crying." She was going to fix my socks and we should all laugh instead. We tried laughing for a while, but the sobs kept tearing through, like hiccups coming from somewhere just above my belly button. Ruthy suggested singing a song, so we all ended up singing "Will the Sun Shine for Me Again," and the mood improved slightly. But late in the night, I could safely return to my irreconcilable misery. The world outside this room seemed like a very uninviting place to be, how and why things were happening was to remain a refractive mystery. Most important, I finally understood that there was nothing, absolutely nothing, in the world that we could do so "they" would love or even like us.

In September, 1943, orders were issued that all Jews above the age of 10 were to wear a yellow Star of David for purposes of identification.

I spent an afternoon sewing the yellow stars on my coat and my black school smock. I used a very strong black thread, the kind you use for stringing beads, to make sure my yellow stars would not get lost. Little drops of sweat crawled down my back when my class-mates looked at me the next morning. Overwhelmed by embarrassment, I pretended indifference and stood quietly behind my bench. After the morning prayer, Sister Josepha covered her silver cross with her fingers and said, "God loves all children." I suspected that she was saying this to me and I felt that the class knew that too. In the yard, hidden behind the wooden steps of the gymnasium, Tatiana and Lilette spent a long time carefully examining my yellow star. They remarked on its good quality, how strongly it was sewn and how well the yellow went with my navy coat. Lilette even volunteered that she wished she had a yellow star too.

Then Lilette said she had a secret, a very big secret, and we would have to swear to rot in hell if we ever opened our mouth! Her father, Dimiter Petrov, was an Anglophile, she said. "And what is an Anglophile?" we inquired. "Somebody that loves the English," she answered, and more, her father heard BBC every night, even last night. Wow! We asked what they said on BBC, but Lilette did not remember, she only thought it was very good. We kept discussing and whispering and that whole affair made us feel so good that we decided to become Anglophiles.

Skipping on my way home, I concentrated on stepping only on the grey stones of the sidewalk. "If I do not step on the light stones I can make a wish." So I wished that God wouldn't change his mind. I then whispered very softly to myself so that only magic spirits could hear: "God loves all children, God loves all children." So as long as I was a child, I was still on the right side. What about adults? How does He feel about all adults? But this lasted only a moment. Being adult was very far away. I abandoned this trend of thought. I had a future, I would be an Anglophile.

THE LAST LIVING JEW

by Elie Wiesel, translated by Lily Edelman and the author

Concentration Camp Fence. Imperial War Museum, London.

This is the story of a ghetto that stopped living, and of a beadle who lost his mind.

It was the beadle's custom to rush to the synagogue each morning, to ascend the *bimah* and shout first with pride, and then with anger: "I have come to inform you, Master of the Universe, that we are here."

Then came the first massacre, followed by many others. The beadle somehow always emerged unscathed. As soon as he could, he would run to the synagogue, and pounding his fist on the lectern, would shout at the top of his voice: "You see, Lord, we are still here."

After the last massacre, he found himself all alone in the deserted synagogue. The last living Jew, he climbed the *bimah* one last time, stared at the Ark, and whispered with infinite gentleness: "You see? I am still here."

He stopped briefly before continuing in his sad, almost toneless voice: "But You, where are You?"

JERUSALEM DAY

If I forget you, O Jerusalem, let my right hand wither.
—PSALM 137:5

Pray for the well-being of Jerusalem;
May those who love you be at peace.
May there be well-being within your ramparts,
peace in your citadels.
—PSALM 122:6

Jerusalem, city of peace! For thousands of years, the very mention of Jerusalem, the sound of those syllables, evoked longing in Jews around the world. For generations, Jews alone, Jews in small groups, and Jews in large influxes have arrived at the city's gates. At the end of the War of Independence in 1948, the Old City, including the Western Wall of the Temple (the *Kotel Ha Ma'aravi*), was under Jordanian rule, and Jews were barred from worship at this holy place. But after the capture of Jerusalem in the Six-Day War in 1967, Jerusalem was returned to Israel and reopened to all. Jerusalem Day (*Yom Yerushalayim* in Hebrew) celebrates the reunification of the city; it is the most recent of Jewish holidays, falling on the twenty-eighth day of Iyar (usually between early and late May).

For the most part, Jerusalem Day is observed only in Israel, but more and more people in the Diaspora are beginning to celebrate it. In Jerusalem, people watch the parade along the main street, attend a craft show, concert, or other performance, and sing "Jerusalem of Gold"—the city's secular anthem, written by Naomi Shemer just before and just after the Six-Day War. Celebrants also visit Ammunition Hill, now a museum— its capture was essential to taking Jerusalem from the Jordanians—or walk on the ramparts of the walls to experience the flavor and history of the city.

Jerusalem Day is a time to reflect: "What is the place of Jerusalem, both ancient and modern, in my heart?" This is the occasion to plan a trip to Jerusalem, find out more about the city, read poetry about it, or "connect" with Jerusalem in some other way. Wherever you are, this may be a good time to read the many stories of ancient and modern Jerusalem and to sing psalms and prayers for the continuity of the city.

Temple at Jerusalem, Mark Podwal, 1996. Courtesy of the artist.

It is an age-old custom to insert small written messages and petitions to God (called kvitlech *or* tzetlech *in Yiddish) into the spaces between the large stones of the Western (Wailing) Wall. According to legend, God's spirit always dwells there. To send a message, you don't have to be in Israel. Merely e-mail your petition: http://kotelkam.com/prayers.htm.*

A New Holiday

Ezechielis. v.

Hæc est Ierusalem, Ego eam in medio Gentium posui, et in eius circuitu terras.

1. Ager Acheldemach
2. Domus mali confilij
3. Natatoria Siloe
4. Cœnaculum
5. Turris Dauid
6. Via quæ ducit in Bethleem
7. Domus Caiphæ
8. Hic B. Maria nutrita est
9. Sepulchrum V. Mariæ
10. Locus, vbi Dauid sepul: cum
11. Domus Annæ, Ionias Psalm:
12. Torrens Cedron
13. Porta aurea
14. Templum Salomonis
15. Sepulchrum Domini
16. Locus Caluariæ

17. Hic Christus flagellatus fuit
18. Probatica piscina
19. Vallis Iosaphat
20. Lazarus
21. Hic S. Stephanus est lapidatus
22. Hoc loci Christus orauit
23. Domus diuitis epulonis
24. Domus Pilati
25. Domus Herodis
26. Palatium regni peregrinorum
27. S. Veronica
28. Locus decollationis S. Ioannis
29. Castrum Pisanorum
30. Locus in quo Petrus amare fle:
31. S. Martha
32. Arcus Pilati

33.
34. Hic Esaias serra diffectus est
35. Fons Rogel
36. Mons Oliueti
37. Mons Sion
38. Cœmiterium Abaßanorum
39. Turris Syloe
40. Vbi B. Maria nata.
41. S. Stephani
42. Porta ——
43. Damascena
44. —— Iudaica
45. Turris Iosaphat
46. Hic se fugit commiserunt Apost:
47. Domus S. Mariæ Magd:
48. Mosquee.

How the Walls of the Temple Were Built

Land of Israel folktale, retold by Howard Schwartz

It was King David who first dreamed of building the Temple in Jerusalem. At night, in his dreams, he would climb Jacob's ladder until he reached the heavenly Jerusalem. For there is a Jerusalem in heaven that is the mirror image of the Jerusalem on earth.

King David was fascinated with the heavenly Temple, which was built at the beginning of time. In his dreams, he studied it from every side. So, too, did he explore every chamber of it. And when he awoke, he would write down the description of the heavenly Temple, for it was his plan to build one exactly like it in the city of Jerusalem.

During his lifetime, King David had the foundation of the Temple dug, but after his death it was up to his son King Solomon to see that it was built. So King Solomon called everyone together—the rich and the poor, the princes and the priests—and he said: "People of Israel, let us build a splendid Temple in Jerusalem in honor of God. And since the Temple will be the holy place of all the people, all of the people should share in building it. Therefore you will cast lots to decide which wall you will build."

So King Solomon prepared four lots. On one he wrote *North*, on another *South*, on the third *East*, and on the last *West*. Then he had each group choose one of them. In this way, it was decided that the princes would build the northern wall as well as the pillars and the stairs of the Temple. And the priests would build the southern wall and tend the Ark and weave its curtain. As for the wealthy merchants, they were to build the eastern wall as well as supply the oil that would burn for the Eternal Light. The job of building the western wall, as well as weaving the Temple's curtains, fell to the

poor people, who also were to pray for the Temple's completion. Then the building began.

The merchants took the golden jewelry of their wives and sold it to pay workers to build the wall for them, and soon it was finished. Likewise the princes and the priests found ways to have their walls built for them. But the poor people, who had no money to pay for workers to help them, had to build the wall themselves, so it took them much longer.

Every day the poor came to the site of the Temple, and they worked with their own hands to build the western wall. And all the time they worked on it, their hearts were filled with joy, for their love of God was very great.

At last the Temple was finished, as beautiful as the Temple on high. Nothing in the world could compare with it, for it was the jewel in the crown of Jerusalem. And after that, whenever the poor people went to the Temple, fathers would say to their sons, "Do you see that stone in the wall? I put it there with my own hands." And mothers would say to their daughters, "Do you see that beautiful curtain in the Temple? I wove that curtain myself."

Many years later, when the Temple was destroyed, only the Western Wall was saved, for the angels spread their wings over it. For that wall, built by the poor, was the most precious of all in the eyes of God.

Even today the Western Wall is still standing. Now it is sometimes known as the Wailing Wall, for every morning drops of dew can be seen on its stones, and it is said among the people that the wall was crying at night for the Temple that was torn down.

And, as everyone who has been there can testify, God's presence can still be felt in that place.

ISRAEL INDEPENDENCE DAY

As long as deep in a heart
The Jewish soul yearns,
And toward the East
Jewish eyes turn toward Zion,
Our hope is not lost,
Our two-thousand-year-old hope
To be free in our land,
The land of Zion and Jerusalem.

—HATIKVAH, ISRAEL'S
NATIONAL ANTHEM

After almost two thousand years of Jewish history, a new holiday was proclaimed: a birthday celebration for the State of Israel! Israel Independence Day, which takes place on the fifth day of Iyar, in late April or early May, does not stand alone but is preceded by Yom Ha Zikaron, Remembrance Day for Israel's fallen soldiers. Yom Ha'atzma'ut, Israel Independence Day, commemorates Israel's military and political victory over its Arab neighbors in the War of Independence and the founding of the new state on May 14, 1948.

In Israel, Yom Ha Zikaron is a solemn day of remembrance for Israel's fallen soldiers. At 11 A.M., a siren's moan brings the country to a two-minute stop. During the day of Yom Ha Zikaron the air is heavy; sadness is everywhere. Television and radio stations broadcast interviews with veterans and with parents and spouses of the fallen. This is a day for visiting graves, reciting Kaddish—the mourners' prayer—and holding a Yizkor service, a memorial for the deceased. Ashkenazi Jews also recite *El Male Rachamim*, a memorial prayer chanted at funerals and during memorial services. Sephardi and Mizrachi Jews have a corresponding memorial prayer called *Hashkavah*.

At the end of the day, the mood changes from one of sorrow to one of festivity. The streets

Israel Independence Day, Michal Meron, 1995. Courtesy The Studio in Old Jaffa, Israel.

A New Holiday

are packed. Flags fly. Lights glow. In the spirit of celebration, thousands crowd the streets, banging one another on the head with plastic hammers or spraying people with colored foam. The next morning, many people pack picnic lunches and prepare for public outings, where they dance, sing, and eat together. Sometimes members of a particular fighting unit organize a reunion. Veterans of every branch of the service reminisce. Songs of the early Zionists, of pioneering days, or of individual fighting units can be heard— *B'arvot Hanegev* ("In the wilderness of the desert [a soldier has fallen]"), "Song of the *Palmach*," and the popular *Babi el Wad*. This is the time for folk dances, fireworks, military parades, air shows, and the Hebrew Song Festival.

In religious terms, the day represents a return to the homeland promised to Abraham when he was instructed to journey there. If one considers that God's hand is always revealed in history, the establishment of the State of Israel is a magnificent act of God. Jews feel they are privileged to build communities in Israel with God in their midst.

Because not everyone can be in Israel on this day, Jews in the Diaspora show solidarity with Israel by participating in public parades, community picnics, and Israeli fairs. Jews everywhere honor Israel by eating Jewish foods, dancing traditional dances, and singing Israeli songs. At the signing of the peace accords at Camp David, the Israeli prime minister read Psalm 126; on Independence Day, it is sung to a popular melody or read at religious services held by Reconstructionist, Reform, and Conservative Jews. Yom Ha'atzma'ut, Independence Day, is a time for Jews outside Israel to reflect: "What is the relationship of the Diaspora with Israel?" and "What do I want *my* relationship with Israel to be?"

The Magen David, or Jewish star, was adopted as Israel's national symbol after the establishment of the state, partly because of its messianic ties. Legend has it that when David, whose family will produce the Messiah, was escaping from the armies of Saul, he ran into a cave to hide; a spider then spun a web in the shape of a star over the cave's entrance. When the pursuing soldiers arrived at the cave, they did not think that David could be inside because he surely would have broken the web; so they turned back, leaving David in safety. Thus the popular phrase "Star of David" was born.

In the Sultan's Pool Looking Up

A memory by Peninnah Schram

Going to Israel is like visiting home. In the summer of 1980, I traveled to Israel for two weeks with a tour group. One night in Jerusalem, when the schedule showed there was free time, I decided to go to the opening concert at the Sultan's Pool, an outdoor amphitheater. Thousands of us were crowded together for the concert. While a few people had brought folding chairs, the majority of the people were sitting on the earthen ground. I, too, was on the ground, although on a bedspread I had "borrowed" from my hotel room. The Sultan's Pool area was actually a scooped out sunken arena, and the ground was still heavily pitted with rocks and stones of all sizes and shapes, none of them rounded. I can assure you that it was not the most comfortable of "seats."

Sabbath in the Kibbutz,
Yochanan Simon,
1947. Collection, Tel
Aviv Museum of Art.

Finally the concert was about to begin. First, Jerusalem Mayor Teddy Kollek addressed us; then the Israeli Philharmonic, conducted by Leonard Bernstein, took the stage.

But the most memorable part of the evening for me came at the beginning of the program after Bernstein had come to the podium. As he lifted his baton for "Hatikva," we all stood up to sing the anthem of "hope." I realized that this was the first time I had actually sung "Hatikva" in Israel. Suddenly I felt the closeness of everybody. Literally, the whole audience was standing shoulder to shoulder. With arms around my new friends standing next to me, we were holding onto each other.

At that moment, I looked up at the stars and everything came together—thoughts and images of my mother and father being there with me in spirit rushed through me. I never felt so much at one with the Jewish people. Tears welled up in my eyes. I had never before seen so many millions of stars, and the words of God's promise to Abraham came into my mind: "Look now toward heaven, and count the stars, if thou be able to count them.... So shall thy seed be" (Genesis 15:5).

I was thrilled, excited, exhilarated. I almost couldn't sing, the experience so took my breath away. And the stars were multiplied many times over through the prism of my tears. At that moment I began to sing louder than I had ever sung before, filled with hope.

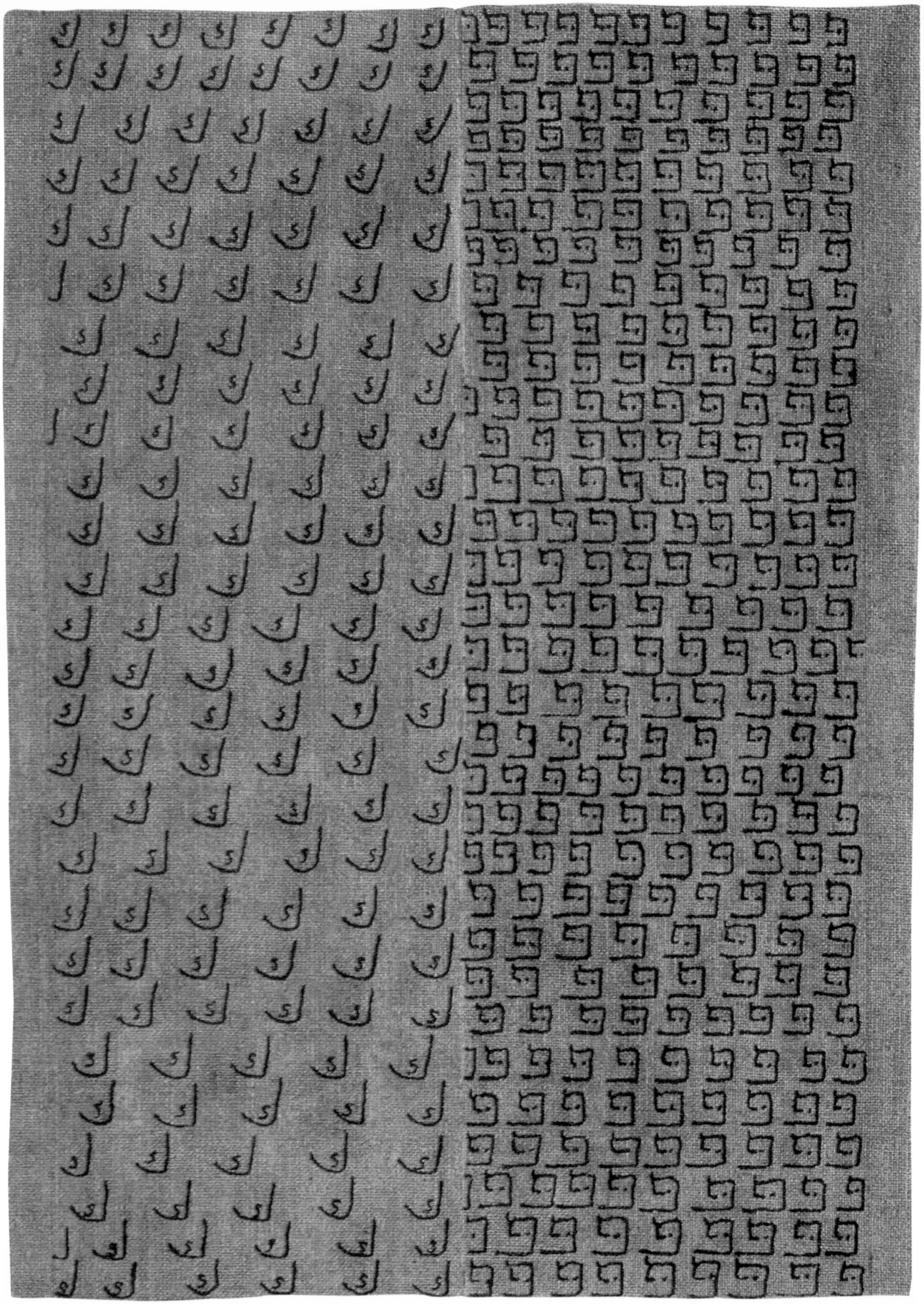

THE BURNING PIANO

by Karen Golden

A Hebraic-Arabic Alphabet, Jane Logemann, 1990-1991. Gift of Tobi Haleen in memory of Michael Rosen. Photograph by John Parnell. The Jewish Museum, New York/Art Resource, NY.

When I lived in Jerusalem, I played my saxophone in a concert band every Wednesday night. One night after practice, a group of us was sitting at the back of the band room packing up our instruments when the conversation turned to Israel's War of Independence in 1948. It seemed like every Israeli over age fifty who was sitting in our little gathering had a story of battle or heroism except for Avraham. He just sat quietly swabbing out his clarinet. "What about you, Avraham?"—all faces were on him. "You must have a story or two." He was such a quiet man. I had never heard him speak before. He adjusted his shirt collar, stroked his graying black hair a few times, and pulled out a stray thread from his sweater before talking in a slow, deliberate manner. "I was only a boy during the war, not much of a hero. I don't even like war. Oh, I'm sorry, that was silly of me to say. None of us likes war—what I meant was, I knew very little about the war. I arrived in Palestine shortly before the war began. It was all so new." Avraham made no eye contact; he just looked down at his clarinet. But then he looked up, and there was a quivering smile on his face. "I guess I do have a story to tell you. It's the story of why I decided to become a music teacher."

We all sat silently and watched him, not knowing how he would link his love of music to the war. The rest of the band members went home except for those of us who were huddled together in the corner trying to hear. Avraham spoke haltingly, in a low, raspy voice. "I was born in Baghdad, Iraq, and lived in a big house with my family, and what a house it was. We had a large, silver vase in the entranceway, many worn books on the bookshelf, and brightly woven carpets on the stone floors. My parents liked nice things. We even had a piano in the big room. I was learning to play when suddenly, we had to leave everything behind, just before my Bar Mitzvah. Life for the Jews wasn't good in Baghdad. We took a few small suitcases and flew to Palestine. It was my first plane ride! When we arrived, they told us there wasn't enough housing and we would have to live in a temporary camp in Jerusalem. It was a tent village. We lived in a tent! They said they would build more houses—stone ones. So we lived in the tent and waited. We had three metal beds and a few wooden chairs.

"There wasn't much to do there. No work for my father or school for me, just a lot of waiting around, trying to learn Hebrew. One night, I was lying in bed when we heard a loud noise outside. It was louder than anything I had ever heard. I knew this was the sound of gunfire. My father pulled me from my bed, and we started running along with my mother and brother. We ran from the tent village and just kept running toward some permanent houses, which were not far from our tents. Then we saw an opened door and we ran into a house. I don't think we knew where we were running; we just ran. My father said it would be safer inside. There was no one home, but there was a meal on the table—pita bread and salad. We left the door open thinking the people would return any minute. At first we waited for them before eating their food, but we were so hungry that we ate everything. There was even a grand piano in the main room, and that night, while we heard the loud noises outside, I played the piano softly inside.

"The next day we went out, and in the daylight we saw that we had run into an Arab village and were in an Arab home. From the inside, we had had no idea it was an Arab house. There were books in Arabic, just like those we read in Iraq. But on the outside of the house was painted a small, black square, which means the family were Moslems and had made the pilgrimage to Mecca. We decided we would stay until the owners came back, even though it gave us a funny feeling to be inside an Arab home. We were afraid to return to the tent because there was no protection. We felt we had no choice but to stay. All of our neighbors were our friends from the tent village. They had all run into open homes.

"The weather kept getting colder and colder. My father couldn't find work, and we had no money. There was very little firewood, and because the house was so big, we burned it all in a few days. We had to burn the furniture to keep warm. We burned all the chairs and tables, but we were still cold. One day, my father came to me with very sad eyes and told me we would have to burn the piano. It was good wood and we would have to burn it if we were to survive the winter. First he burned the bench, then the legs and the top. I could still play it until he burned the body. Then there were just strings lying on the floor, which wouldn't burn. They were useless strings, not good for anything but to serve as a painful reminder of how vulnerable we really were. It hurt me to think that our lives had come to this: using a piano as firewood. I felt as if a part of myself had been destroyed. I decided at that moment that I would become a music teacher to bring music out of wounded hearts once again. I would teach people that the purpose of a piano is for warming the heart, not the house. This is my story of the war. By the way, the people never came back to their houses. I guess I wasn't a hero, but I do have this story. It has lived within me every day of my life."

When Avraham finished, we sat there silently. No one could think of anything to say. We just picked up our instruments and went home.

When I lived in Jerusalem, I used to love going to the old city, especially to the Shuk (market) to experience "sensory overload." First, there were the smells: baking bread, spices, and sewage. Then there were all the bright colors, from Persian rugs to shiny brass coffee trays, and finally there was the symphony of sounds: people talking, mezzuins calling the Moslems to prayer, and church bells ringing. I never felt afraid to walk anywhere in the old city—even the Moslem quarter felt safe. Perhaps it's because I'm an American that I felt I could cross into this world without fear.

I had a favorite shop, not far from the Damascus gate, which was owned by an Arab man named Ibrahim. His store was like a tiny cave peeking out from under the street. It was filled with artifacts that he collected from the wandering Bedouin peoples: brightly colored pink and purple embroidered dresses, carpets, hangings, even camel saddles! Ibrahim always had a smile on his face, with two gold teeth sparkling in the front. He was a small, balding man who moved with childlike agility through the nooks and crannies of his little shop. Whenever I went to visit him, he would brew up a pot of strong tea over a small, open fire, which he lit inside a metal pot. We sat on handmade wicker stools, and he always told me stories about his customers from all over the world. He was proud of the fact that he knew people from almost every country, and he would point admiringly at the many photographs of his international customers that were all over his shop—even on the dress hangers.

After the first few sips of tea, Ibrahim would pull out a huge scrapbook, at least a foot thick, filled with smiling photos, letters, quotes cut out of different kinds of documents, and newspaper clippings. On one such visit we were looking at the scrapbook when he said, "Blease, read this letter. It is filled with much Beace." He couldn't pronounce his "p's," and his English was filled with many mistakes, but he always spoke without hesitation. "You mean 'Peace'?" He laughed. "Yes, beace, I mean peace." I unfolded a well-worn sheet of blue stationery and read out loud: "Dear Ibrahim, we love our Bedouin carpet; it reminds us of your little

shop and our visit with you. We have enclosed our five favorite poems about peace for your scrapbook, as promised. We also told our neighbor Nelly, and her poems and picture will be in the mail next week. We wish you much strength. Love, Hans and Ingrid." Next to the letter were five short poems written out longhand on white paper and a picture of Hans and Ingrid standing with Ibrahim.

He flipped through the pages. There were letters written in languages I couldn't read, and many poems and quotes, such as "Peace begins with me" and "Peace, not war." The scrapbook was overflowing and loose papers kept slipping out onto the floor. One letter was from 1953! "When did you start your peace scrapbook?" I asked.

"After the war," he said. Then he laughed. "I wish after the war—it is still going on. I mean after the big one in 1948, when I was a child. I started my scrapbook when we lived in the little houses, the refugee camp. At first everyone was very angry and people said bad things all the time. The word *hate* was in almost every sentence. Once I heard my friend say something about being peaceful. I was so happy I said, 'Mohammed, will you write what you said on paper? I want to keep it.' He thought I was joking so he just wrote it and laughed.

"I kept the paper in a little notebook and thereafter, anytime anyone said something nice, I told them to write it down. My book was quite thin for a long time because people didn't say nice things very often. But then it started to grow. Whenever my friends found a poem or quote about peace, they copied it and gave it to me. I showed my

book to all the people in my village who were especially angry about our move. They called me the dreamer, but at least they laughed!"

"Move—what move?" I asked.

"The move from the village of my birth in Jerusalem . . . not really a move . . . we all ran away out of fear. It was a warm spring day. The sun had gone down and we were waiting for my father to come home from work. It was getting so late that we were worried. My mother put the dinner on the table, pita bread and salad . . . . I was helping her roast a chicken in the outside stove when we heard a very loud noise and saw flames in the sky. My mother screamed, and then my father came running toward us. I don't know to this day who told us to leave or why—they just kept yelling, 'Run, run!' So we started running—we ran from our beautiful house.

"And what a house! It was made of stone, not like the little houses we ran to, which were made of old boxes and tin. Our house was so big we even had our own yard, filled with olive trees and grapevines. Our house was so big that when the piano played in the main room, it rang out like what I imagine the voice of Allah to sound like. Did I ever tell you about our piano? I used to play the piano, but after we moved I never played again. We never went back—all gone, all gone. This is why I started my scrapbook, to make music with words and people's hearts. When I read these words of beace, I hear music in my heart."

Ibrahim showed me one final letter that day. It was in Yiddish, from an old friend of his father. "My father spoke Yiddish with an Arab accent. He had many Jewish friends before the war. He wrote to these friends until he died, but he never saw them after the war. He just couldn't . . . . But I saved the letters as proof that we can all be friends." I finished my tea and thanked him for a lovely afternoon. Ibrahim kissed me on both cheeks and said, "May Allah be with you."

I heard both of these stories within a year of each other, but I never thought of them as a single story until I came back to the United States to live. One sunny afternoon, I was thinking about my life in Israel and the many people who had crossed my path. Somehow, I thought about Avraham and Ibrahim. Perhaps it was because they both have the same name. I was awestruck when I realized that their lives may have been connected by the same house and the same piano, as well as the same war, the same sorrow, and the same redemption. These two Abrahams have fulfilled God's prophecy by making their lives a blessing.

And the Lord said to Avram, get out of your country and from your kindred and from your father's house and go to a land that I will show you. And I will make of you a great nation and I will bless you and make your name great and you will be a blessing. (Genesis 12:1-2)

SHAVUOT

*hen you shall observe the Feast of Weeks for the Lord your
God, offering your free will contribution according as the Lord
your God has blessed you.*

—DEUTERONOMY 16:10

*...For wherever you go, I will go; wherever you lodge, I will
lodge; your people shall be my people, and your God, my God.*

—RUTH 1:16

In spring, in the days of the Temple, people brought baskets laden with the first harvest of wheat, barley, olives, dates, pomegranates, grapes, and figs (Deuteronomy 26:1-5) to the altar. Two loaves of leavened bread, made from choice crops, were offered in thanksgiving by the priests. Shavuot, sometimes called Holiday of First Fruits and celebrated on the sixth of Sivan, is the shortest of the pilgrimage festivals to the Temple. It is celebrated for one day in Israel and by Reform and Reconstructionist congregations in the Diaspora, and for two days by Conservative and Orthodox congregations in the Diaspora.

From biblical times until the first century C.E., Shavuot was a festival for farmers. But after the destruction of the Second Temple in 70 C.E., the rabbis saw Shavuot as the continuation of Pesach: the political liberation from Egypt culminated in the spiritual revelation at Sinai. And so Shavuot became the "time of the giving of the Torah"—*Z'man Matan Torateinu*—at Sinai

(Babylonian Talmud: Shabbat 86b). Although the Bible establishes no link between Moses going to Mount Sinai and Shavuot, and no specific date is given for the event, Shavuot has become the anniversary of the day on which the Law was first revealed (that is, the Ten Commandments and, in some traditions, the oral law as well, were given to Moses) and a covenant was concluded between God and the people of Israel (Deuteronomy 4:2; 13:1).

This covenant is not a one-time agreement; it is a continuous relationship between the people and God. Just as the agricultural harvest recurs from year to year, the historic experience at Mount Sinai is renewed as well. Each person there heard the voice of God. At Mount Sinai, the Jewish people were given and accepted the Torah; from that moment, every Jew became a mutually dependent partner with God in making the world perfect. Today, on Shavuot, each individual remembers the historic event, and each reaffirms commitment to Torah.

Shavuot: The Harvest, Harry Lieberman, 20th century. The Jewish Museum, New York/Art Resource, NY.

The Feast of Weeks

Book of Ruth (detail), Shalom of Safed, c. 1970. The Jewish Museum, New York/Art Resource, NY.

A Chasidic tale asks, "Why is Shavuot called Time of the Giving of the Torah and not Time of the Receiving of the Torah?" The answer is that Jews were given the Torah on that day at Mount Sinai, but they continue to receive the Torah.

On Shavuot, the home and synagogue are full of beautiful greens; roses are scattered everywhere. According to midrash (biblical interpretation), the Israelites fainted from fear and awe when God began to utter the Ten Commandments; God then revived them with roses and spices. Another midrash reveals that Mount Sinai was covered with trees and green grass, as is alluded to in Exodus 34:3—even though, in reality, the area is

desert. The scattering of greens probably derives from an Eastern European Christian festival that took place around the same time as Shavuot. The Gaon of Vilna, an eighteenth-century Jewish religious leader, prohibited Jews from copying the Christian custom of scattering greens and flowers. So in the Ukraine and parts of Poland and Russia, Jews began instead to cut and display paper in floral shapes.

To celebrate at home, Jews light two candles, perhaps to symbolize the two tablets received by Moses. Blessings recited are *Ner shel Yom Tov—* "the light of the festival"—and *Sheh-heh-cheh-ya-nu,* as well as the blessing over the wine—*Borei pri*

Cheese—eaten as blintzes or burekas—is a popular dish on Shavuot, perhaps because this spring festival is a pastoral one, celebrated when cheese is ripened and ready for eating. Or the eating of cheese on Shavuot may recall the Israelites' return from Mount Sinai, when they were too hungry to take the time to slaughter animals, check the knives, and cook the meat according to the new laws they had just received.

hagafen. Yahrzeit candles are lit in memory of deceased parents and grandparents.

The Shavuot challahs are not the ordinary loaves eaten on Sabbath. On this day two loaves are joined together so that the two sides are touching—resembling the two tablets of the Law—a symbol often found in folk art. Perhaps the two challahs represent the zodiac sign of Gemini (twins), the sign of the Hebrew month of Sivan.

It is said that at midnight on the first night of Shavuot, the heavens open for just a moment, and a wish made at that moment will be granted. This is the time when people beseech God for an end to barrenness, illness, and other problems. And because God is easier to reach on this night, the mystics of Safed made it a time of continuous study of portions from every book of the Torah and Talmud. According to midrash, however, there is another reason for this all-night vigil: the Israelites overslept on the morning that they were to go to Mount Sinai and had to be awakened by Moses. To atone for their sleepiness, Jews now stay up all night. The night is called *Leil Tikkun*, Hebrew for "the night of repairing" (participating with God in repairing the world).

At the synagogue, joyful celebration marks Shavuot. Exodus 19 and 20, which tell of the giving of the Torah and the presentation of the Ten Commandments, are read during the service. Each person "grasps" the Torah as the scroll is passed from one to another. Jews of North Africa stage a symbolic wedding procession with a wedding contract (*ketubah*) between Israel (the bride) and God (the groom), and the Torah scroll is dressed in white, as is a bride.

The story of Ruth, a Moabite woman who embraced the faith and people of her Jewish mother-in-law (that is, accepted the Law), is read on Shavuot. Midrash points out that the central characters, Ruth, Naomi, and Boaz, performed acts of kindness (*chesed* in Hebrew) beyond what was necessary; one lesson of the Book of Ruth may be that law is not enough—the world also needs loving-kindness.

The ceremony of confirmation, when teenagers in Reform congregations agree to follow the Law, is held on Shavuot, as are the adult Bar and Bat Mitzvah ceremonies (another symbolic accepting of the Law) in other congregations. It is a time for all Jews to ask themselves, "What commitments of Torah study am I willing to take on? What deeper meanings can I find in the Ten Commandments?"

The festival of Shavuot honors three sacred Jewish spaces: the Temple of ancient times, the synagogue of today, and the cemetery. Like other major festivals, Shavuot is a time for remembering the deceased. In the synagogue, the Yizkor service is held, and memorial candles are lit. Kurdish Jews take fruit to the synagogue to be blessed in memory of the dead. Other Jewish groups go on pilgrimages to the shrines of holy men and women.

King David, author of the biblical Psalms, is said to have been born and to have died on Shavuot. Sephardi, Mizrachi, and Ashkenazi synagogues have their own liturgies for the Psalms, which give thanks for God's revelation in history and nature.

THE TORAH OF MY SERVANT MOSES

A Yiddish tale, retold by Beatrice Weinreich

This is the story that Reb Joshua ben Levi tells concerning the time when the Holy One, blessed be He, gave the Torah to Moses, peace to his memory.

As Moses was descending again from Heaven, Satan came to the Holy One, blessed be He, and said, "Lord of the Universe, where have You hidden the Torah?"

The Holy One, blessed be He, replied, "I gave it to the Earth."

Satan went to the Earth and said, "Earth, where did you hide God's Torah?"

The Earth replied, "God knows everything. But as for me, I don't have the Torah."

So Satan went to the Sea and said, "Sea, where have you hidden the Torah?"

The Sea replied, "I don't have it."

So Satan went to the Abyss and said, "Where have you hidden the Torah that God gave you?"

The Abyss replied, "It's not in my depths."

Then Satan went to the dead and to those who are lost and asked them, "Where have you hidden the Torah?"

They replied, "It's true that we have heard of it, but we don't know where it is."

So Satan went to God and said, "I've searched the entire world over and have not found the Torah."

The Holy One, blessed be He, said, "Go to Ben Amram—to Moses, son of Amram. I gave it to him."

So Satan went to Moses and said, "Moses, where is the Torah that God gave you?"

Moses replied, "Who or what am I that the Holy One, blessed be He, should have given the Torah to me?"

When God heard about this, He said, "Moses, why did you deny that I gave you the Torah?"

Moses replied, "Lord of the Universe, how can I take it upon myself to boast that it is I who have received the Torah, an instrument which produces such joy that studying it makes all humankind happy every day?"

God said, "Moses, Moses, it is not well to belittle oneself. Still, because you would not boast of having the Torah, let your reward be that it will henceforth be named after you."

And so it is written, "Remember the Torah of My servant, Moses...."

Moses Receiving the Ten Commandments On Mount Sinai from the Sarajevo Haggadah, (fol. 30), 14th century. The National Museum of Bosnia Herzegovina, Sarajevo.

WHY JEWS EAT DAIRY FOOD ON SHAVUOS

Eastern European folktale, retold by Barbara Rush

Eastern European
Jews as depicted in
The Abyss of Despair,
17th century.

In the city of Vilna, the Jerusalem of Lithuania, there were women scholars versed in the holy books. Once a furor was raised by the renowned righteous woman, Fruma, the wife of Rabbi Leib: "Until when? Is it right that the Torah should imply, 'And he will rule over her' [Genesis 3:16] and that we should stand idly by and keep silent? An end to this! We must amend the verse to read, 'And she will rule over him.'"

In the large women's gallery, a meeting of women took place. Most of them had no idea what was being said, but they wiped tears from their eyes and declared: "Fruma the righteous is right!" In short, the shriveled women of Vilna suddenly took up the cause of women's rights.

Fruma urged that they invoke a strike during the coming holiday of Shavuos*. Yes, let the men taste a holiday that lacked the labor of their wives! It was agreed that during the holiday no woman would dare cook or bake. And the women did as they had planned. As the holiday approached, they dressed in lovely clothes, did not toil in the kitchen, did not prepare fish, did not cook meat, and did not bake bread. In short, a strike of protest, with its slogan being "And she will rule over him," had begun!

After prayers, Rabbi Leib returned home, and what did his eyes behold? The table was not set. His wife, Fruma, was on strike—on the holiday, of all days!

In order to calm down, he lit his pipe (it is permitted to smoke on Shavuos) and went outside to breathe some pure air. Rabbi Leib was walking near his house when he noticed that other heads of households were also out walking.

"Happy holiday!" said Yankel the wagon driver.

"What kind of happy holiday?" answered Yasha the porter. "My old woman has gone mad. She hasn't prepared any food."

"Oy, my old woman has also lost her mind," said Yankel.

The other heads of households soon realized that this was not an individual matter. The men understood that if they were dealing with a women's revolution, the instigator could be none other than Fruma, the wife of the rabbi.

"And what is the rabbi's opinion in this matter?" they asked Rabbi Leib.

The rabbi ordered that Fruma be summoned; she came at once, accompanied by six additional housewives.

"What is this strike?" asked the old rabbi of his wife.

"We, the women, demand the elimination of the harsh law, 'And he will rule over her.' It must be amended to say, 'And she will rule over him.' If you men refuse, then, with all due respect, go and be housewives yourselves!"

With his eyes shut tightly, the old rabbi listened to his wife's complaints. "Correct, correct! But we men also have demands. If this strike does not end at once, we will cancel the injunction of Rabbenu Gershom, Light of the Exile, who forbade a man to take more than one wife. From this time onward, every man will have the right to marry one—or more—additional wives."

Upon hearing this, the wife of Rabbi Leib became as pale as whitewash, and ran off with the rest of the women to prepare for the holiday. And because they had neither fish nor meat available, they grabbed what was readily at hand: a piece of dough from here, a slice of cheese from there, and so they made blintzes.

From then until this very day, the custom of preparing dairy foods on Shavuos has remained. And the world still accepts as its practice the biblical ruling, "He will rule over her."

*The pronunciation in Eastern Europe.

TISHA B'AV

Alas! Lonely sits the city once great with people!

She that was great among nations is become like a widow...

—LAMENTATIONS 1:1

Take us back, O Lord, to Yourself, and let us come back;

Renew our days as of old!

—LAMENTATIONS 5:21

"In the month of Av, all merriment goes out," religious sources tell us. Tisha B'Av, which falls on the ninth of the month, is a day of universal mourning.

Why such sadness and gloom? This holiday, which literally means the ninth of Av, or Ab (falling in either July or August), is a day for remembering the destruction of the two Holy Temples in Jerusalem: the first by King Nebuchadnezzar of Babylonia in 586 B.C.E.; the second by Rome in 70 C.E. Although the destructions did not occur exactly on the ninth day of Av, it is the day officially designated for mourning. If Tisha B'Av falls on the Sabbath, it is postponed for one day.

Av was not always a month of sadness; at one time it was the month of a joyous vineyard festival. But later, rabbis searching Jewish history for reinforcement of the idea that the ninth of Av is a day of mourning, found other tragedies that occurred then. In ancient times, the Children of Israel refused to enter the Promised Land on this day and were thereby condemned to wander in the desert for forty years. On this day in 135 C.E., the Romans captured the last stronghold of Simeon bar Kochba, the commander of the Jewish rebellion

Menorah from a Mahzor (Ms 8236), Corfu, 17th century. Courtesy of The Library of The Jewish Theological Seminary of America.

A seven-branched gold menorah, originally fashioned by Moses, accompanied the Israelites in their wanderings. Later a similar menorah was kept burning in the First and Second Temples. Today, this major Jewish symbol is part of the emblem of the State of Israel.

Remembering the Holy Temples

The Coming of Elijah from *Washington Haggadah* (fol. 19v), Italy, 1478. Library of Congress.

against the Romans. During the Middle Ages, in the year 1190, the Jews of York, England, were slaughtered on this day; and exactly one hundred years later the remaining Jews were expelled from the country. The Jews of France were imprisoned (and then expelled) on Tisha B'Av in 1305. In modern times, the Arabs attacked the Jews of Palestine on this day in 1929, and in 1942, Nazis deported the Jews of Warsaw to Treblinka. All these occurrences lend sadness and solemnity to the day.

The *Zohar*, the greatest work of Jewish mysticism, tells us:

> When the sanctuary was destroyed and the Temple was burnt and the people driven into exile, the Shechinah left her home in order to accompany them into captivity. Before leaving, however, she took one last look at her House and the Holy of Holies, and the places where the priests and the Levites used to perform their worship....(2:134a)

With the destruction of the Temples, not only the people but also God's presence was believed to go into exile. Therefore, for weeks before the holiday until the actual day of Tisha B'Av, there are signs of mourning: no marriages, no haircuts or new clothing, and no listening to or performing of music. Mourning customs gradually increase as Tisha B'Av approaches: people show no sign of joy, consume no meat or wine, and do not wash or bathe. Just before the start of Tisha B'Av, Jews eat a meal of mourning, consisting of hard-boiled eggs or lentils, the foods traditionally consumed in a house where a death has occurred. Bread is dipped into ashes. (Throughout the Bible, ashes are associated with grief and mourning.) Then both men and women observe a twenty-five-hour fast. As on Yom Kippur, they do not wear leather shoes and do no work.

In modern times, Tisha B'Av has been interpreted in many ways. Some consider it a time for mourning the victims of the Holocaust. Others see it as a day of remembering non-Jewish victims of Hiroshima and Nagasaki, a catastrophe that, like the destruction of the Holy Temples, occurred during the summer months. Still others view Tisha B'Av as a time for reaching out to all refugees, people in exile, as Jews once were.

The *Zohar* also says:

> So in the days to come, when the Holy One, blessed be He, will remember His people, the community of Israel, the Shechinah will return from exile first and proceed to her House, as the Holy Temple will be rebuilt first.

The rabbis tell us that only those who mourn the destruction of the Temple will merit the privilege of seeing it rebuilt; and so, on this day, Jews relive the devastation and experience the grief of exile. Inside the synagogue, the ark, *bimah* (prayer platform), and Torah scrolls are often draped in black; no light is lit; a hushed aura fills the room. The Book of Lamentations is read aloud, mourning the destruction of the First Temple. In some synagogues, the Torah is placed on the floor and sprinkled with ashes. The congregation recites, "The crown has fallen from our head. Woe to us that we have sinned" (Lamentations 5:16). Or before the reading of Lamentations, the shofar is blown, as in Temple times, when wailing mourners in sackcloth, also a sign of biblical mourning, threw themselves down before the altar.

A special prayer book containing dirges and elegies is used, and scriptural passages are read. Kaddish is recited. There are no signs of joy; no tallit (prayer-shawl) or tefillin (phylacteries) are worn; ashes are placed on the forehead. In the afternoon, study is permitted, but only of passages dealing with catastrophe and mourning, such as the Book of Job.

Usually, defeats such as the destruction of the Holy Temple mean the collapse of an entire nation. Not so with Judaism, for it is the Jewish way to turn a sign of defeat into an omen of salvation. To mourn a death is to assert rebirth. And so Tisha B'Av, the day on which Jews mourn the destruction of the Temples, has also become the date on which the Messiah will be born. Disaster and desolation lead to hope and renewal.

By late afternoon, at the Mincha service in the synagogue, the mood changes to one of joyous welcome for the Messiah. In Libya, young boys would ride donkeys, hoping to meet the Messiah (who, it is believed, will arrive on a donkey). Today, in many synagogues, the words "Renew our days as of old" are repeated several times by everyone present, a hopeful phrase beseeching that as the Jewish year is ending, and a new one about to begin, God will make our days full of newness!

After sundown, the fast is broken, and people wash and attend a hallowing-the-moon ceremony. As the moon is renewed on Tisha B'Av, so too will the Jewish people be renewed.

Scroll of Fire

by Hayim Nachman Bialik, translated by Ben Aronin

All night long the flaming seas had boiled and tongues of fire had spread themselves above the Temple Mount. Stars sprang off the heat-seared vault of heaven and earthward poured bright flames on flames. Had God then spurned His throne and shattered His own crown to bits?

And shreds of reddened clouds laden with blood and fire strayed in the vast, vast spaces of the night, recounted there among the far-off mountains the raging of the God of Vengeance and told His wrath among the desert rocks. Had God then rent His royal robe and scattered to the wind its fragments?

And there came the terror of God upon the distant mountains and a trembling seized the sullen desert rocks: the God of Vengeance, the Eternal One, the God of Vengeance shone forth!

Behold the God of Vengeance, Himself in all His glory calm and awesome, sitting on a throne of fire in the heart of a sea of flame! His robe is purple flame and His footstool burning coals. Leaping flames have encompassed Him. A cruel dance burns around Him. Upon His head flame rages, gulping greedily the void of the world. And He, calm and awesome, sits with His hands against His heart. He causes the flames to spread with the glance of His eyes and deepens the fire pits with the movement of His lids. Give glory to the Eternal, O dancing flames, give glory to the Eternal, O dance of flame and fire!

And when dawn blossomed on the mountains and pale mists stretched in the valleys, then did the seas of flame grow silent and the tongues of fire sink down from the burnt Temple of the Eternal, upon the Temple Mount. And the ministering angels had gathered as was their custom in choruses of Holiness to sing the song of dawn. And they opened the windows of the firmament and inclined their heads full toward the Temple Mount to see if the Temple doors were opened and if the cloud of incense smoke ascended. And they saw, and behold the Eternal, the God of Hosts, Ancient of Days, sitting in the morning twilight over the desolation! His garment was a pillar of smoke and His footstool dust and ashes; His head bowed low between His arms and mountains of sorrow on His head. Silent and desolate, sitting and gazing at the ruins, His eyelids darkened with the rage of all the worlds and in His eyes congealed was the Great Silence. And all the Temple Mount still smoked hills of ashes, hills of embers and smoking brands were massed together, and whispering coals in heaps and heaps, sparkling like mounds of carbuncles and rubies in the stillness of the dawn.

And the Lion of Fire had couched upon the altar always, day and night, even he—extinguished, one orphaned lock from his mane's edge flickering, trembling and expiring on the heap of burnt stones in the stillness of the dawn. And the ministering angels knew what God had done to them, and they trembled exceedingly, and all the stars of morning shuddered with them, and the angels veiled their faces with their wings, for they feared to look upon the sorrowing of God.

And their song was turned that morning into silent lamentation and a thin still wailing. Silently they separated and wept, each angel by himself, and all the world in silence wept with them. And one soft sigh, soft and deep, arose from the end of the earth and spread itself and was shattered into a muted weeping. The heart of the world was broken, and God no longer could restrain Himself. And the Eternal awoke and roared like a lion and smote His hands together, and the Shechinah arose from over the ruins and went into the hidden places.

Tisha B'av, from *Sefer Minhagim*, Amsterdam, 1723. Courtesy of The Library of The Jewish Theological Seminary of America.

THE MESSIAH'S OVERCOAT

by Aaron Sussaman

My grandfather picked me up and cradled me in his arms, letting my head rest on the bushy gray pillow of his beard. I had stayed up late to listen to him and the other men in the study house of the synagogue tell stories about the Messiah, and now I was so sleepy I could hardly keep my eyes open.

He carried me outside into the night, wrapping part of his overcoat around me for a blanket, and headed down the long, moonlit hill toward his house. It was like being curled up in a bed that was slowly bobbing along high above the world.

I closed my eyes and thought of the stories, full of sweetness and ache, that I'd heard. I loved the one about how the soul of all the Jewish people sat with the Messiah in his palace, waiting with him, her grave eyes, like his, seeing to the end of things. I loved best of all my grandfather's own story about how God took the moon away from the world for one day, and the world wept because until then it didn't know what need it had of the moon—that was how the Jews would weep, and be lost, if the hope of the Messiah were taken away for even one day.

I could hear my grandfather, as though from far off, singing me a lullaby in Yiddish. It was a song about what the world would be when the Messiah came. What good things to eat and drink, what wisdom from King Solomon, what music from King David, what stars in the sky, like eyes that shine with tears when the joy of the heart overflows.

The Rabbi and his Grandchild, Mark Gertler, 1913. Southampton City Art Gallery, Hampshire, UK/Bridgeman Art Library, London/New York. Courtesy Estate of Mark Gertler.

The button on my grandfather's coat that had been rubbing gently against my forehead, like a little secret wanting inside, got quieter and quieter and finally grew still. I fell asleep.

There, in his arms, I dreamed of the Messiah. He looked like my grandfather, but he glowed. He was sitting on a cloud, smiling, because God had just told him that it was time to put on his overcoat and come down to earth. So he stood up and he put on his overcoat and he started buttoning the buttons. I became very sad. I looked at all the buttons he had to button, and it seemed to me there were more of them than stars in the sky. I was sure it would take him forever to finish.

When I awoke, my grandfather was tucking me in bed. "Grandfather," I asked, muddled with sleep and innocence but wanting so to understand, "why does the Messiah have to wear an overcoat when he comes? Can't he just come in his pajamas?"

My grandfather smiled softly, giving the ancient, wistful shrug of the wise, and kissed me good night.

"To every thing there is a season, and a time for every purpose under the sun."

ECCLESIASTES 3:1

The Hebrew Calendar

The Year:

The Jewish year, recorded on its own special lunisolar calendar, is determined by the 365 days of the earth's revolutions around the sun; its twelve months (of twenty-nine or thirty days each) are determined by the moon. The years are reckoned from the time of creation in 3761 B.C.E.; and so, to calculate the Jewish year that corresponds to any Gregorian year, merely add 3760 to the Gregorian year. Thus, the year 2000 will equal 3760 + 2000, or 5760 on the Hebrew calendar.

The Months:

The months on the Hebrew calendar have different names and differ in lengths than those on the calendar we use in our secular lives. When the calendar was created in biblical times, people were agriculturists, and they marked the time of year by season rather than month. For example, the dry season was April through September, while the rainy season extended from October through March. The twelve months had no names, and were referred to as "the first month," "the second month," etc. But upon the Jews' return from Babylonia in the fifth century, Jewish months were given names similar to those of their Babylonian counterparts.

There is a discrepancy of approximately eleven days between the total of 354 lunar days of the Hebrew calendar and the 365 solar days in the Gregorian one. If the Hebrew calendar were used without any adjustment, the seasonal holidays would eventually occur at the wrong time of year. Thus, hundreds of years ago, the rabbis, who were knowledgeable in both astronomy and mathematics, compensated for this difference in the two calendars by periodically adding an extra month of thirty days, creating a thirteen-month year. In a period of nineteen years, the additional month is inserted seven times (in the years 3, 6, 8, 11, 14, 17, and 19) between winter and spring, between the months of Shevat and Adar; the already existing month of Adar is then called Adar II.

Festival Days:

Traditionally, the profane (not holy) days of the week are unnamed in the Jewish calendar, and are called "the first day," "the second day," and so on. The sacred seventh day, the Sabbath, has its own name: *Shabbat* in Hebrew or *Shabbos* in Yiddish.

In most cultures festivals occur from morning to night; in Judaism, they occur from night to day. According to the Bible, "there was evening and there was morning, a first day" (Gen. 1:5). Therefore, every festival begins on the evening before the festival day and ends at nightfall of the festival day.

The rabbis applied a complex system of rules and formulas to the calendar so that the holiness of the Sabbath would never be desecrated. For example, the carnival-like festival of Purim never falls on the Sabbath. Nor does Yom Kippur, the holiest day of the year, fall on Friday or Sunday, the days preceding or following the Sabbath.

Babylonian	Hebrew	Length	Time of Year	Festival
1. Nisanu	7. Nisan	30 days	March-April	Pesach, Holocaust Day
2. Ayaru	8. Iyar	29 days	April-May	Israel Independence Day, Lag B'Omer, Jerusalem Day
3. Simanu	9. Sivan	30 days	May-June	Shavuot
4. Du'uzu	10 Tammuz	29 days	June-July	
5. Abu	11. Av	30 days	July-August	Tisha B'Av
6. Ululu	12. Elul	29 days	August-September	
7. Tashiru	1. Tishri	30 days	September-October	Rosh Hashanah, Yom Kippur, Sukkot, Shemini Atzeret, Simchat Torah
8. Arahsamnu	2. Heshvan	29 or 30 days	October-November	
9. Kislimu	3. Kislev	30 or 29 days	November-December	Chanukah
10. Tebetu	4. Tevet	29 days	December-January	
11. Shabatu	5. Shevat	30 days	January-February	Tu B'Shevat
12. Adaru	6. Adar	29 days	February-March	Purim

CREDITS

(Within the credits, IFA numbers refer to the Israel Folktale Archives.)

Compilation copyright © 2001
by Fair Street Productions
and Welcome Enterprises, Inc.
Text copyright © 2001 by Barbara Rush

Produced by Fair Street Productions
and Welcome Enterprises, Inc.
Project Directors: Deborah Bull,
Hiro Clark Wakabayashi
Editor: Deborah Bull
Designer: Jon Glick
Production Coordinator: Elizabeth Kessler
Art Research: Photosearch, Inc.

Published in 2001 by
Stewart, Tabori & Chang
A division of Harry N. Abrams, Inc.
115 West 18th Street
New York, NY 10011

Library of Congress Cataloging-in-Publication Data
Rush, Barbara.
    The Jewish Year : celebrating the holidays
/ Barbara Rush.
    p. cm.
ISBN 1-58479-030-X
    1. Fasts and feasts~Judiasm~Legends.
2. Jews~Folklore. 3. Legends, Jewish. 4. Fasts
and feasts~Judaism. 5. Judaism~Customs and
practices. I. Title.

BM690 .R87 2000
296.4'3~dc21
                                00-029718

Printed in China

10 9 8 7 6 5 4 3 2 1

First Printing

"The Pious Cow," retold by Barbara Rush. From *Bet Hamidrash: a Collection of Short Midrashim and Stories of Ancient Jewish Literature* (Hebrew), by Adolph Jellinek. Bamberger and Wahrmann, Jerusalem, 1938. Used by permission of Barbara Rush.

From: "The Kerchief" by S.J. Agnon, translated by I.M. Lask, from *The Jewish Caravan* by Leo W. Schwartz. Copyright 1935, © 1963, 1965 by Leo W. Schwartz. Reprinted and abridged by permission of Henry Holt and Company, LLC.

"The Taste of the Sabbath Meal," retold by Barbara Rush. (IFA 6494, told by Z. Rabin and IFA 7839, told by Shimon Yodi from Afghanistan); based on the Babylonian Talmud, Shabbat 119a. Used by permission of Barbara Rush.

"A Closet in the Wall," retold by Barbara Rush.

"Challahs in the Ark," retold by Rabbi Zalman Schachter-Shalomi. Used by permission of Rabbi Zalman Schachter-Shalomi.

"Capturing the Moon in Chelm," retold by Barbara Rush from the classic tales of Chelm. Used by permission of Barbara Rush.

"Origins of Rosh Chodesh," an original midrash by Penina V. Adelman. Used by permission of Penina V. Adelman.

"The Most Precious Thing in the World" by Joan Sutton. Used by permission of Joan Sutton, Storyteller.

"Fireflies in the Ghetto," retold by Barbara Rush. (IFA 2361, told by Chaim Dov Armon.) Used by permission of Barbara Rush.

"Before" by Penina V. Adelman. Used by permission of Penina V. Adelman.

"The Tale of the Ram" © Rabbi Tsvi Blanchard. Used by permission of Rabbi Tsvi Blanchard.

"From Bad to Worse," retold by Nathan. Ausubel. From *A Treasury of Jewish Folklore*. Edited by Nathan Ausubel, Copyright © 1948, 1976 by Crown Publishers, Inc. Reprinted by permission of Crown Publishers, a division of Random House, Inc.

"An Arab Shepherd Is Searching for His Goat on Mount Zion" ©Yehuda Amichai. Used by permission of Yehuda Amichai.

"The Clever Judgment," retold by Barbara Rush. (IFA 445, told by S. Hilles.) Used by permission of Barbara Rush.

"A Tale of Reb Nahum Chernobler and a Tikkun" (an alternate solution), retold by Eve Penner Ilsen. Used by permission of Eve Penner Ilsen.

"When the Rains Return," adapted by Cherie Karo Schwartz. (IFA 9229, told by Yosef Statya.) Used by permission of Cherie Karo Schwartz.

"Thanks to God Who Gave Us the Toyre," retold by Barbara Rush. (IFA 1648, told by Haim Schwartzbaum.) Used by permission of Barbara Rush.

"A Chanukah Miracle," retold by Barbara Rush. (IFA 3486, told by David Cohen, who heard the story from his grandfather, Reb Pinchas, the hero of the story.) Used by permission of Barbara Rush.

"The Fourth Candle" by Mara (Beckerman). Adapted from a story by Curt Leviant. Used by permission of Mara Beckerman.

"A Tu B'Shevat Miracle," retold by Barbara Rush. (IFA 10103, told by M. Attias.) Used by permission of Barbara Rush.

"The Purim Gift" by I. B. Singer. "The Purim Gift" from In My Father's Court by Isaac Bashevis Singer. Copyright © 1966 by Isaac Bashevis Singer. Copyright renewed 1994 by Alma Singer. Reprinted by permission of Farrar, Straus and Giroux, LLC.

"On Purim" © Rabbi Rami M. Shapiro. Used by permission of Rabbi Rami M. Shapiro/www.simplyjewish.com.

"A Letter to God," retold by Barbara Rush (IFA 5519, told by B. Arabi.) Used by permission of Barbara Rush.

"The Rabbi and the Inquisitor," retold by Nathan Ausubel. From A Treasury of Jewish Folklore. Edited by Nathan Ausubel, Copyright © 1948, 1976 by Crown Publishers, Inc. Reprinted by permission of Crown Publishers, a division of Random House, Inc.

"Seder Night in Bergen Belsen: 'Tonight We Have Only Matzah' " ©Yaffa Eliach, Hasidic Tales of the Holocaust (Vintage Books/Oxford University).

"A Journey to Jerusalem," retold by the North American Conference on Ethiopian Jewry. Reprinted by permission of the North American Conference on Ethiopian Jewry.

"Eliyahu the Prophet" by Sholom Aleichem. Translated by Aliza Shevrin. Used by permission of Aliza Shevrin.

"Rabbi Shmuel the Candle Lighter," retold by Barbara Rush. (IFA 558, told by Zusha Lurya.) Used by permission of Barbara Rush.

"A Star-Crossed Childhood, The Conversion" ©Rosy Abelson. Used by permission of Rosy Abelson.

"The Last Living Jew" by Elie Wiesel as it appeared in Gates to the New City: A Treasury of Modern Jewish Tales (New York: Avon Books, 1983) Copyright ©1983 Elie Wiesel. Reprinted by permission of Georges Borchardt, Inc., for the author.

"How the Walls of the Temple Were Built," from Next Year in Jerusalem: 3000 Years/ Jewish Stories by Howard Schwartz, copyright © 1996 by Howard Schwartz. Used by permission of Viking Penguin, a division of Penguin Putnam Inc.

"In the Sultan's Pool Looking Up" © Peninnah Schram. Used by permission of Peninnah Schram.

"The Burning Piano" by Karen Golden © 1995. Used by permission of Karen Golden.

"The Torah of My Servant Moses." From Yiddish Folktales by Beatrice Weinreich-Silverman, translated by Leonard Wolf. Copyright ©1988 by YIVO Institute for Jewish Research. Reprinted by permission of Pantheon Books, a division of Random House, Inc.

"Why Jews Eat Dairy Food on Shavuos," retold by Barbara Rush. (IFA 388, told by C. D. Armon.) Used by permission of Barbara Rush.

"Scroll of Fire" by Hayim Nachman Bialik. Dvir Ltd. Publishing House, Tel Aviv, Israel.

"The Messiah's Overcoat" by Aaron Sussaman, as it appeared in Gates to the New City: A Treasury of Modern Jewish Tales, edited by Howard Schwartz, © Avon Books.

Biblical excerpts from the JPS Hebrew-English Tanakh, ©1999 are used by permission of The Jewish Publication Society.

The author also thanks and acknowledges the following writers, whose books were essential to the research of this project: Penina V. Adelman, Abraham Ben-Ya'akov, Abraham P. Bloch, Judith B. Fellner, Theodor H. Gaster, Philip Goodman, Eliezer Marcus, Abraham E. Millgram, Chaim Raphael, E. G. Richards, Lesli Koppelman Ross, Hayyim Schauss, Peninnah Schram, Howard Schwartz, Rami Shapiro, Michael Strassfeld, Joshua Trachtenberg, Alan Unterman, Arthur Waskow, and to various Reform, Conservative, Orthodox, and Reconstructionist prayer books.

ACKNOWLEDGMENTS

*This book is dedicated to my parents, Abraham and Sarah Wishengrad,
and to my husband's parents, Morris and Irene Rushefsky, all of blessed
memory, for whom the Jewish festivals were a vital part of their past
and their present, and a gift to us for our future.*

This lovely volume would not have been possible without the help of so many people, to whom I am most grateful: first, to Professor Dov Noy of the Hebrew University of Jerusalem, my mentor and friend, whose loving guidance and vast knowledge have always been available to me, who first taught me to see the festivals through the eyes of the great family of Jews across the world, and who was kind enough to read the introduction and parts of the manuscript.

Many thanks to Rabbi John S. Friedman for reading parts of the manuscript and for sharing the Yom Kippur custom, to Cherie Karo Schwartz for sharing Passover information, and to Simone Lipman for sharing the Alsatian Sukkot custom; to the following, for supplying and clarifying information: Karen Dinur; Fred and Ingrid Hertz; Lew Romer; Eliezer Sagi; Dr. Chaya Gavish, Hebrew Union College, Jerusalem; Dr. Sheva Zucker, Duke University; Rabbi Richard Hirsch, Reconstructionist Rabbinical College, Philadelphia; and Gila Bartur, Dr. Dov Gavish, Professor Raphael Israeli, and Dr. Susan Lazinger, all of the Hebrew University of Jerusalem; and to those who supplied behind-the-scenes logistical help: Professors Marjorie Rosenthal, Peninnah Schram, and Howard Schwartz.

Thanks to the many talented artists and writers whose works grace these pages, and to the archives, museums, and collections from which these works were selected; particular thanks to Dr. Haya Bar-Itzhak, Academic Director, and Edna Hechal, Coordinator, Israel Folktale Archives, University of Haifa, Israel. The editors especially thank Gerhard Guitroy at Art Resource, Havva Charm at The Library of The Jewish Theological Seminary of America, New York, and Susanne Kester at HUC Skirball Cultural Center and Museum, Los Angeles.

A well of thanks to the extra-special people at Fair Street: to Susan Wechsler, who first had the vision of this book; to Deborah Bull, my editor, who breathed every word of the manuscript with me and whose wisdom, imagination, flexibility, perseverance, and cheerfulness were my constant companions in this project; to Shaie Dively, whose sunny voice greeted me on many a phone call; and to Joanne Polster and Gia Forakis, who doggedly tracked down all the permissions. I am grateful to the talented people at Welcome, especially to Jon Glick, whose beautiful design brought the book to life, and to Liz Kessler for all her hard work and insight.

And, very, very special thanks to Don Rush, my partner and friend in life, whose patience and encouragement, whose research and technology skills, accompanied me on every step of the book's journey.